Teaching
the Dead Bird
to Sing

Teaching the Dead Bird to Sing

LIVING THE HERMIT LIFE
WITHOUT AND WITHIN

W. PAUL JONES

PARACLETE PRESS
BREWSTER, MASSACHUSETTS

Library of Congress Cataloging–in–Publication Data

Jones, W. Paul (William Paul)
    Teaching the dead bird to sing: living the hermit life without and within / W. Paul Jones.
        p.   cm.
    Includes bibliographical references.
    ISBN 1–55725–303–X
     1. Jones, W. Paul (William Paul) 2. Catholic Church—United States—Clergy—Biography.   I. Title.
    BX4705.J674A3 2002
    248.4'7—dc21
    2002008367

10 9 8 7 6 5 4 3 2 1

Published by Paraclete Press
Brewster, Massachusetts
www.paracletepress.com

Printed in the United States of America.

To the countless hermits
who populate our hills, towns, and cities.
Invisible, unknown, unrecognized,
they are blessed with the courage to face
the demons,
without and within,
on behalf of us all.

"I would soon go down into the silence."
—Psalm 94:17 (Grail)

"My one companion is darkness."
—Psalm 88:19 (Grail)

"Deep calls to deep...."
—Psalm 42:7

"The soul knows for certain
only that it is hungry."
—Simone Weil, Waiting for God

"The experiences called to mind here
were born in the desert
that we must not leave behind."
—Albert Camus, The Myth of Sisyphus

"You called, you shouted,
and you broke through my deafness.
You flashed, you shone, and you dispelled my darkness.
You breathed your fragrance on me;
I drew in breath and now I pant for you.
I have tasted you, how I hunger and thirst for more.
You touched me, and I burned for your peace."
—Augustine, The Confessions

Contents

Prologue

I once lived in a third-floor apartment in the inner city, within an easy roar of the interstate. Shortly after dawn one morning, I heard a scratching outside my window. It was a mourning dove inspecting the window ledge for immediate occupancy, with infants allowed. She permitted my discreet voyeurism, and soon her venture into motherhood became a centering point for my days. The ledge, having met her specifications, became a foundation sufficient for one nest with one egg.

My grand-bird-daughter was born unceremoniously one morning. I was unprepared for the responsibilities. This city is notorious for early springs that coax the flowering trees into full array, only to be ravaged in midcareer by freezing rain. We were one postnatal week into such a spring when the radio threatened "plunging temperatures." I spent a restless night—me in my warm bed on one side of the window, and my Madonna-bird-friend in the freezing rain on the other.

I awoke with delight to her cooing. All was well. With a smile, I peeped around the window blind and peered into the dawn light. In the corner of the windowsill, she had propped upright her small infant-bird—frozen. With patient repetition, she was trying to teach the dead bird to sing.

Not long afterward, I applied for a nine-month leave from my seminary teaching. For reasons that I am still attempting to discern, I felt driven to enter my own frozen springtime. I would become a hermit for a time. I would perch on some lonely sill, with only myself for companionship. I would be patient this time. I would not fly. Then, perhaps, I could be discovered by One capable of teaching me to sing an untimely song in an unlikely place.

1

Pilgrimage Toward the Desert's Edge

It has been a long pilgrimage for me—from my roots in Appalachia to Princeton University, from United Methodist pastor to Roman Catholic priest, from social activist to Trappist monk, from gregarious extrovert professor to hermit in the Ozark hills. This pilgrimage has been strange, and wild.

Central within that pilgrimage were two particular immersions in monastic life. The first occurred during three months I spent in a monastery in Colorado in 1979. The next was nine months in an Ozark monastery from 1986 to 1987. This book focuses on this latter segment of time.

This is how it began. In the summer of 1971 I took a sabbatical leave from seminary teaching. This was thirty years ago. And God began tearing apart my plan for the rest of my life. Being part of a politically and spiritually involved commune, I had chosen to spend the sabbatical studying the phenomenon of communes throughout the country. Learning of my study, a friend suggested that I explore a monastery. Honestly, I was not even sure those seemingly medieval structures existed any longer. But they do. The pleasant voice on the telephone suggested a weekend. I went.

As it turned out, the nearest Trappist monastery was just on the other side of the mountain from our cabin, cupped in the hands of a high, lush valley. My initial curiosity turned out to be a serious immersion. Three days was all it took. For several months after my return, I struggled to sift through that experience for clues as to why it had impacted me so powerfully.

I returned to teaching, and my fall seminary schedule was heavy enough for the monastic experience to be pushed aside. Actually, I suspect now that the intensity of my busyness may well have been a nervous uneasiness. I was not about to let anything confuse my professional vocation, for which I wanted to believe my life thus far had prepared me. Yet the seeds had been planted, deep enough for them to persist. But they were sowed on marginal ground. It would be seven years before I risked coming near a monastery again.

My life's journey began in a tiny coal-mining town in Appalachia, the weathered company houses propped uneasily on stilts against the mountainside. The only color was a yellow creek, smelling of sulfur leakage from the mines. Many miners never exited the mines alive; others were injured for life; but none of us escaped being branded in some way. There was little here to attract anyone to monasticism.

I discovered early that there are two ways out of Appalachia—death and scholarships. Football, the preferred way, was impossible for me, a skinny runt of a kid. Academic scholarships, rarely used, were my hope—

encouraged by a father who had finished the third grade. This implausible pilgrimage from Appalachia led through a junior college housed in a former elementary school to three graduate degrees at Yale. Although I had largely shelved the conservative Protestant upbringing of my youth, I remained plagued by the question of "why" with regard to everything. This led me from literature, to philosophy, and finally to theology. After six years of teaching at Princeton University and a sabbatical year in France, I moved my family halfway across the country to Kansas City. Instead of teaching *about* Christianity, I became intrigued with becoming the philosophical theologian at a new United Methodist Seminary. I would thereby be forced to teach and thus live from *within* a Christian perspective— whatever that might turn out to mean.

In 1971, the year after the Kent State turbulence, my wife, five daughters, and I took a further step. We sold our suburban home and bought a tenement house in Kansas City, intending that the plight of the poor would be our own plight as well. Theologizing was coming to mean participating in those arenas of change where we would most likely encounter the Spirit's moving. Several friends joined us, ten in all, and we formed an intentional Christian commune called Kauchema Community (meaning "to celebrate"). We located the community on the top two floors of the tenement house, with the first floor made available as inexpensive housing for the poor.

It was in the second year of the community's existence that we visited intentional communities around the country as part of the sabbatical, sharing ideas, models, and experiences. It was during this time that I was introduced to monastic life.

As I look back on that time, I am as surprised as I am fascinated. Our experimental community actually had the anatomy of a monastery. This was probably due, in part, to a member who was a former nun. We had morning and evening prayers, reserving one room with big pillows for a diversity of liturgies, with each member taking a turn in leadership. We celebrated a weekly Eucharist. All things were held in common, including finances. We maintained an emphasis on caring for the poor.

Our community lasted seven years. It ended when a majority of members felt the need to expand this alternative approach with experimental living of their own. My direction was toward a revised version of the dream in and through monasticism. One step in that direction was a cooperative arrangement between the seminary and a Benedictine monastery. They sent students from their rural setting to work with us in urban exposures, while our seminary, in turn, sent students to them to participate in monastic life.

I see better now how the convergence of these factors began to make the Trappists attractive to me. Seven years after my initial involvement with the monastery in the Colorado Mountains, I could put off the yearning no longer. I asked permission to enter the monastery again, this time for three months. As I had both hoped and feared, the experience so marked me that I felt a need to make the deeper experience available to others. The book that resulted was *The Province Beyond the River: The Diary of a Protestant at a Trappist Monastery.*[1]

I have often asked myself, and have been asked, what I discovered during these monastic months of formation. Three things in particular seem to have laid claim to my imagination. The first was *silence*, as it surrounded and invaded me. Each evening the silence became a tangible darkness. The second claim was *the daily Eucharist*. Each morning at daybreak, through the Eucharist we were gifted with one more amazing day. How different was my experience of the Catholic mass from the Protestant four-times-a-year Communion of my youth, when attendance dropped by half. Perhaps it was the mystery that lured me most—when the earthy breeze and clouds and sounds at every open window intertwined with the common-day bread and wine of our living. Or perhaps it was the rhythm of offering the whole of creation into God's becoming, and receiving it back, graciously blessed for the daily journey. Or maybe it was that in each Eucharist, Calvary and the Resurrection became renewed as the rhythm of all time. During the liturgy, my imagination was flooded with a kaleidoscope of imagery. With the death dance in our blood, we washed each morning the feet of the world. And at Compline each evening, we returned the day to God, and in the lonely darkness participated with joy in God's ongoing suffering on behalf of the universe. "Into your hands, Lord, I commend my spirit."

The third claim made upon me by monastic life was *a slowing down of the pace of living.* Inevitably one is force-fed to take time for life by becoming clearer about priorities. In the monastery, doing emerges out of being, and being becomes the reason for doing. And the intersection of these three claims gradually opened still a fourth claim. The best name I know for it is *ecstasy.* While it began then, I have come to understand it as a spirituality most available for extroverts. This made clear to me why for much of my life I could never affirm myself as spiritual. Much of the spirituality I knew had come from introverts, beginning with my introverted parents and then with the monks, many of whom are introverts. Not surprisingly, then, almost all of the extensive reading I was assigned insisted that contemplation is the highest form of prayer, serving as the center of mature spirituality. Here, one loses one's self in God, much as mystics do in a deeper sense.

Gradually I became convinced that this is only one approach to spirituality and thereby should not be regarded as necessarily the highest form. Rather, this is the type of prayer life that comes most naturally for introverts, and would presumably be the highest form of spirituality *for them.* While being open, even desirous, for the unlikely possibility of losing myself in God, at the heart of what I have learned is a spirituality more natural for extroverts. In time, all I had to do was look in any direction from the monastery. I experienced myself frolicking as a colt in a lush meadow chalice formed by mountains on all sides. The river, the early morning mist, the deer feeding at evening, eagles riding the high winds, wild flowers in every color imaginable, the taste of wine at silent meals, the smell of baking bread—everywhere the ecstatic dimensions of life began emerging as grace-filled gifts.

I remember one morning in particular. Standing by a stream in a misty meadow of wildflowers, I remember feeling sorry for Moses, whose seeing was restricted to only one burning bush. This was the beginning of what would become increasingly powerful in my understanding though the years. The spirituality particularly available for extroverts centers in the joy of being encountered by Presence, in and with and through almost anything—a trickling stream, a full moon, the creativity of a mockingbird, even the tick of an aging clock. Yes, anything, everything. Rather than losing one's self, it is as if the self is being interpenetrated with things and persons. It is like greeting and being greeted as an invasion of promise. It is a primal way of living the essence of Christianity—as the religion of hope, with monasticism the foretaste of that future.

Previous to this time, I would never have said that I had experienced God. Yet something happened one day as I gazed out of my window at the rising sun reflected on the snow-peaked Mount Sopris. I heard myself finally able to say yes to the question phrased this way: "Have you ever experienced life as a gift from God?" "Oh, yes!" Then came a deeper question: "Have you ever participated in the becoming of God?" I knew, then, that sooner or later this would become my final question, maybe as a persistent whisper. At this particular moment I might have been close to saying yes. This question would follow me into my desert adventure. It had to do with the ability to affirm that everything all around me is incarnation—and thus the very immanence of God.

If I remember my elementary grammar course correctly, this was the time when I began to live in the subjunctive—*as if*. But it was still only an invitation. I needed more—an ongoing, formative relationship with a Trappist monastery. However, the one in the Colorado Rockies was eighteen hours away from Kansas City. After much searching (for they do not advertise), I found a monastery in the Ozark Mountains, only five southerly hours away. Here I was drawn into my nine-month immersion, preparing for and living as a hermit. It is with that adventure that some of the journal entries of this book are concerned. I kept these journals as a way of coming to understand and appropriating in some more definitive way the delicious terror that would be awaiting me in the desert.

Before focusing on that period, however, I need to share several things of importance that give shape to the intervening years between the three-month Colorado immersion (1979) and my adventures as a struggling Ozark hermit (1986–87). One of the most important of these was my divorce, based amicably on the honest discernment that the mutual pilgrimage of my wife and myself had reached a divergence. Her choice ventured down the path toward feminist witchcraft, mine toward monastic spirituality. Nevertheless, marriage is rooted in the making and keeping of promises. This was reinforced by my emerging theology that we are to live our Christian faith as a foretaste of the Divine promises. Therefore I needed to keep my own. So while we no longer live together, we mutually support each other and celebrate special days together. And although our five daughters are dispersed about the country, each year we find sacred stability in spending Christmas together at my hermitage. Ironically, when through divorce my promise was no longer legally obligatory, it became absolute—because I had given my word.

In addition to the divorce, both of my parents died during this period. My mother died of a broken heart over my choices regarding the spiritual and political direction of my life, as well as over my divorce. Then three months later my father was defeated by cancer.

Only after the death of both parents did I enter into full connection with the Roman Catholic Church. Although for me it seemed a natural step in my pilgrimage, my parents never would have been able to endure it, given their Protestant background and their attitude toward Catholicism.

My experience was different. Surprisingly, the first two books assigned by the novice master for my formation were the writings of Macarius the Egyptian and those of Bernard of Clairvaux. These two were at the top of John Wesley's list of favorites. He was the founder of Methodism, the church that had been my religious home in Appalachia. I began to appreciate the significance of the fact that Wesley's high-church orientation likely would have been Catholic if the

Church of England had not split from Rome more than two hundred years before. As a youth I found Wesley's creativity exciting, but I was disappointed over how little of this foundation remained. One can understand my surprise and delight, then, in experiencing the Trappist monastery as seeming to incarnate much of what characterized the Wesleyan movement. The Trappist approach to the spiritual renewal of Catholicism was amazingly close to Wesley's efforts at spiritual renewal for Anglicanism. In seeing this, I had to admit: I have a Protestant mind and a Catholic heart. So did Wesley.

The deep similarities between Trappist and Wesleyan practices included daily Eucharist, spiritual direction, a *lectio divina* approach to Scripture, extensive intercessions, covenant promises, small groups for support and accountability, and concern for the imprisoned and the poor. Strange as it seems, it was a Roman Catholic monastery that was birthing in me the life that Wesley expected of the serious Christian. This was why it felt natural for me to take the next step—living out the ecumenical tradition into which I had been unknowingly born, and with which I was now being monastically formed. I hoped that by being faithful to both traditions my lifestyle might make a tiny contribution to ecumenical renewal.

While I will always be a child of the '60s, I grieved during the '70s when many of my radical friends abandoned the dream of social justice. Becoming fatigued, they were lured by promises of the "good life." Strangely, what was happening to me was a rebirth through disillusionment. The entrance ticket into monastic spirituality was a thought gleaned from Karl Barth: *Success is not in my hands but God's; my call is simply to be faithful.* But faithful to what? At this point an intellectual crisis I had had during my theological studies at Yale reemerged, this time as a passionate commitment. Convinced then that there would have been no Christianity without the Resurrection, in all honesty I needed to confess that a dead man could not rise from the dead. Yet, not long afterward, I awoke one morning to a striking shift in the issue. No longer was the question whether Jesus rose from the dead. Rather, it had become this: What difference would it make if Jesus *did* rise from the dead? What emerged was my first taste of faith as wagering one's life on the *resurrection vision:*

> *Then I saw a new heaven and a new earth. . . . And I
> heard a loud voice from the throne saying, "See, the
> home of God is among mortals. He will dwell with them;
> they will be his peoples, and God himself will be with
> them; he will wipe every tear from their eyes. Death will
> be no more; mourning and crying and pain will be no
> more, for the first things have passed away."*
> (Rev. 21:1, 3-4)

But I had tried *myself* to make this dream a reality. Disillusionment was inevitable. What I lacked, if I was to stay the course, was a spiritual foundation for living faithfully this Christian vision in the face of never-ending defeats. *The vision is God's.* Mine is to be faithful to that Divine

Promise, drinking from the chalice lifted on behalf of Appalachia and beyond. And yet, waiting creatively for the definitive action by God entails living *now* as if the Kingdom is already here—in a lifestyle of foretaste. Thomas Merton, in his final lecture delivered hours before his tragic death, claimed for himself the same dream as I, reaching the same conclusion. If the Christian vision is realizable, Merton stated, it would be in the monastery as foretaste. Monasticism, having existed as long as the Church itself, entails a long period of formation and transformation, with the absence of all private property and ownership as a test at the center. Above all, the monk is striving to make common cause with the early church. "Now the whole group of those who believed were of one heart and soul, and no one claimed private ownership of any possessions, but everything they owned was held in common. . . . There was not a needy person among them" (Acts 4:32,34).

Finally I understood that this was a powerful reason for my being drawn into monasticism. The monastery's intent, structure, and dynamics are truly a valid counter-cultural option, making realizable some of the best features of the 1960s. But while the average existence of hippie communes was five to seven years, monasteries measure their existence in terms of centuries. While contemporary society tends to pit persons in an either/or posture of win/lose, monasticism is intent on re-forming persons so that they are motivated through community into the cooperation of a both/and posture of win/win. And whatever failings particular monasteries may evidence, what I find most appealing is their coherence of words and action, altar and pulpit, being and doing, work and leisure, silence and sound, outer and inner, fast and feast, self and community, promise and foretaste, realism and hope.

Since my nine-month desert adventure over a decade ago, to which we are about to turn, my pilgrimage has brought me ever closer to being able to drink deeply the promise of the Christian vision.

Above all, it has been this hermitage and its land where I now live that has provided the foretaste. I am clear about when I am most with God. It is through the cocreativity of a poem well-crafted, a piece of hickory finely carved, a soup of sprightly vegetables, the smell of a freshly cut cedar log, the soft touch of the morning mist, a sunset well seen and applauded. My hermitage is sacred, nestled in the intimate greenness of a cedar forest. It had its birth as doodles in the margins of agendas for boring faculty meetings. I wrongly assumed these sketches were simply a method for preserving sanity. Over the months, however, the margins began to exhibit variations on a common architectural design.

During this same time, apparently as a way of balancing the urban intensity in which I was living, I took weekend camping trips. On one of these, I was touched by the solitary gentleness of a particular lake. Responding to a strong urge, I left the campground, took the blacktop road to the first dirt road on the left. In ten minutes I was at the end of the road, skipping rocks from a ledge, and knowing that this piece of land would become home.

As a child of the Great Depression, I learned how to make almost anything out of an orange crate or its equivalent. As an adult, however, I become almost immobilized by the presence of a purchased piece of fine wood. My solution was to develop an agreement with a company that demolished condemned tenements in my neighborhood. I agreed to help them in return for salvageable lumber and all the bent nails I could carry away. Each weekend the pile of accumulated lumber at the lake grew, and my mantra became the sound of a hammer unbending nails.

I was not sure why I was building this place. Yet it seemed as if the building was building itself, each part with its own hidden reason for being. I was most encouraged when, after its completion, persons who knew me well insisted that walking into this hermitage was like walking into my soul. Now as I write this, I am taking a hard look around the inside of the hermitage. It seems that one of the major principles involved is my love of openness. The windows are large, with the interior divided by function rather than walls. A second principle would seem to be a love of creativity as surprise, evidenced by multiple angles. There are hardly any predictable squares, so that the whole is designed as an invitation to explore on the inside what can hardly be guessed from the outside—much like the human soul. And at the center is a fireplace visible from everywhere on the main floor, reflected as well by windows into the sleeping loft, where the moonlight plays with blossoms at the windows serving as a greenhouse.

During the five years after its completion, I experienced a gradual disclosure of the reason why I was led to create this place. And the next major step in my spiritual pilgrimage turned out to be the largest of my life, and it would depend on the ability of what I had thought was a cabin to function deeply as a hermitage. Experiencing myself as a dead bird, in 1986 I took an academic leave, left the city, and entered the Trappist monastery in the Ozarks. At such crucial times as this, it does not seem that I am the one making the decisions. I felt as if I were being lured in such a way that I could not say no. The abbot, who was to become my spiritual director, arranged for me to receive several months of formation at the monastery, until I dared to live the rest of the nine months as a hermit in my own hermitage.

This is the crucial time, happening over a decade ago, on which the journal entries in this book center. While I have been able to describe my life fairly clearly up to this point, it is only because I have the advantage of hindsight. The nine months to which I now turn is the fulcrum from which my whole past has gained its clarity, and my future its meaning.

❦

Obviously, I have hesitated for a long while before permitting this story to be published. As you enter the desert with me, my uneasiness will become more understandable.

This account requires that I disclose my vulnerability, confess my weaknesses, share my secrets, and expose the insecurities of my fragile soul. Yet in the years since, I have discovered how many of us have hermit souls—known or unknown, self-conscious or not. In fact, the life most of us live is a lonely one, wandering through our own wildernesses, eager to find a traveling companion with whom we can be vulnerable together, as we traverse the yellow brick road.

So with you, the reader, I dare now to share my story. It includes before and after, but focuses primarily on those strange and marvelous nine months. Through the encouragement of friends, I do so as a friendly beckoning from the other side of the desert, to you who might be on the near edge. I am reminded of a sermon by the Scottish preacher, Arthur John Gossip. He preached it on the Sunday following the sudden death of his wife. It is entitled, "But When Life Tumbles In, What Then?" Gossip ends with the analogy of "standing in the roaring of the Jordan, cold to the heart with its dreadful chill, and very conscious of the terror of its rushing." And yet he concludes: "I can call back to you who one day in your turn will have to cross it. Be of good cheer, my [friends], for I feel the bottom, and it is sound." I know best the desert and its torturous silence. I know, too, that each of you will likely be called someday for desert duty. And on that day, you must enter the barren wasteland alone, with your life in your hands. To refuse is to doom oneself to fleeing for one's life, going the wrong way. My message is akin to Gossip's. Speaking as one hermit soul to another, "Be of good cheer, my friends, for there are oases along the way."[2]

2

The Desert In Retrospect

My crucial nine-month experience, first at the Trappist monastery in the Ozarks and subsequently in my own hermitage, ended January, 1987. I returned to the city, intent simply on resuming my teaching and social justice work, only to discover that I could never again return to "normalcy." The nine-month desert experience had so claimed me that I realized there had been no closure after all. What was required was that I now reenter the adventure, returning to the hermitage—the sacred place that has become my soul's home. Thus at the completion of the spring academic term, only four months after I thought my desert pilgrimage had climaxed, I find myself again seated in my hermitage at my sloped monk's desk, looking out through the large front window toward the lake. I know now at this point in my pilgrimage that I am being driven to make sense out of last year's raw attempts and failures as a hermit, laying hold of the hints of success. Somehow I must complete the frightening task of discerning and appropriating the fullness of that strange experience, figuring out what truly happened back then. During these next three months, my thinking and my feelings, which have not always been on speaking terms, must learn to embrace each other. Since the way I learn best is through action-reflection, I dutifully journaled throughout my desert experience. Now, to bring closure to that learning, I am taking this summer to reflect in solitude. What I am writing is really a retrospective journal—journaling as a way of appropriating my original journal. As I now pore over the entries from those nine months, I see how much my pilgrimage was truly a "desert experience," as our early Christian fathers and mothers would call it.

And as I begin writing now, I know two things for sure. First, this desert experience has led me to the threshold of a major conversion. Second, for the serious searcher, entering the silence is essential—a silence for which the hermit will always stand as symbol and model.

Sunday, May 10, 1987

A gentle spring day is blowing itself in through the open hermitage door. On a cedar limb right outside, a cardinal is very red against a very blue sky. Notes, journal pages, and mementos from my nine-month pilgrimage clutter every flat surface. For several days I have been reading them, sorting them, reading them again, trying to find a beginning place that makes most sense out of the whole.

The foundational question is worth taking some time to ponder: Why on earth did I even want to enter the harsh solitude of a hermitage? It seems as though I had a deep need to

*discover if my life had a fundamental plot, or was my extroversion
simply excessive sound and needless fury to cover the nothingness. During the past week, I have had a recurring dream. I am
in a forest, replete with magical creatures as helpers. Together
we battle something that is outside, lurking in the shadows. But
the more we struggle, the more it seems that whatever is in the
shadows already has entered deeply inside of me. The darkness
without and the darkness within—this may turn out to have
been the theme of my desert search.*

Friday, May 15

*After struggling for five days, this morning a structure for
my desert experience begins emerging, almost as if it were a
book. The dead bird story could well function as a Prologue.
Chapter One would be concerned with what happened in my
past, giving substance to me as the person who entered the
monastery as preparation. Here I would need to confess my
self-doubts and uneasiness as to whether or not what I was
doing made any sense. A second chapter would be an honest
confession that my first efforts at the hermitage were a total failure. Then, just as plays have intermissions, so did my journey.
Three weeks of travel that I feared would be an intrusion and
distraction, instead provided a broader context into which my
desert experience became part of a larger whole.*

*Chapter Three would center on my return to the monastery
for additional formation, sufficiently important for me to give
hermiting a second try. Chapters Four and Five would be the
centerpiece, for it is only then, all alone in my hermitage, that I*

truly enter the crucible of silence. There the desert confrontation finally occurs. That is when the shadows outside disclose their home base inside, creeping in through every window and door. "Desperate" might be the best word to characterize the disposition of this period. There is a powerful parallel here with the scriptural story of Jacob wrestling with the angel, through which tradition teaches that in the desert one wrestles with God until one is blessed with a new name. In the hermitage, my wrestling was with an Absence until it was God, too, who became renamed in the struggle. Then a final chapter would center on a Christmas closure at the monastery, a Christmas extending as well into my hermitage. Finally, and perhaps hardest of all, I would need a Postscript, distilling how my life in the present is issuing forth from that desert experience.

And what is the overall plot of this story of mine? My hunch is that as I figure this out in the months ahead, it will have something to do with trying to run from a nonexistent God, only to be so burned by the Absence that it becomes the only Presence that matters.

Tuesday, May 19

Yesterday, I jumped ahead of myself in the story. So back to basics. Is there more to be said about the why of the hermit experience? If the seeds were not actually planted in me by Henry David Thoreau, he certainly understands.

> *I went to the woods because I wished to live deliberately, to front only the essential facts of life, and to see if I could not learn what it had to teach, and not, when I came to*

*die, discover that I had not lived. I did not wish to live
what was not life, living is so dear.*[1]

I am convinced that Thoreau is not much different from
the rest of us. A friend recently sent me an article from an air-
line flight magazine. The summary in the margin, intent on
enticing the reader, reads: "We all need a sanctuary to which
we can escape from the clamor and distractions of daily living—
where, in the healing touch of quiet, we can reduce life to its
basics." My pilgrimage turned out to require more than that
author suggests—more than "a chair, a candle, and some spot
reserved for the inconsequential." Yet the author's intent is close
to mine: "Not to miss the important in the unimportant—such
as sunrise and sunset, snowtime and springtime." Yes.

I recall Ed Hays's understanding of how hermits and
hermitages can be made available in any home.[2] He suggests
setting aside an afternoon or day each month in a place desig-
nated as holy space. Furnished in stillness, away from all
duties, the only items proper to enter with us are such things
as Scripture, spiritual reading, drawing materials, or sewing.
The primary temptation that is most likely to confront us is to
ruin the experience by doing work. The healing that we all
need depends on remaining there alone, doing nothing.

I recall having had such a "hermitage of the heart" when
I was a boy. Probably we all did. Mine was on the third limb of
a very unique apple tree. There I could cry, compose poetry,
nurse wounds, and fantasize the rest of my life. It would have
helped had I known then what I know now—that there are
many of us out there, sitting somewhere, alone in the silence,
doing what I did.

Saturday, May 23

After a restless night, I arise with the awareness that there are more reasons than I acknowledged for the decision to enter into the hermitage experience. It might well have been an older-life crisis, as I had entered my midfifties. That was about the time that I began thinking about life in shorter gulps. The future as a delaying tactic for hiding the present became less convincing. With less and less time out in front of me, I felt forced finally to come to terms with me, before it was too late. I entered the night and the silence of hermit life *in order to get rid of the burden of me.* That is as honest as I can get!

Wednesday, May 27

I have been trying to identify more exactly the process I used to force an introduction of me to myself. It is one of removing everything but me, *until I become the desert. It is in having only myself for company that the silence becomes a serious nightmare. I recall a confrontation in a faculty meeting some years ago. I proposed having a compulsory four-hour period of silence and solitude during the orientation time for new seminarians. The professor of pastoral care and counseling was furious: "If we do this, you will be personally responsible for any psychological breakdowns!" He was concerned with the damage that several hours alone could do. And here I am (was) at that very point, measuring the upcoming silence by months.*

Monday, June 1

As I make coffee this morning, I become aware that this distinctive period of my life that I am exploring has serious roots going back over a decade. Although I was trained in some of the finest universities, and taught theology for twenty-five years at some of the best schools, I must make this confession. For much of my life I have been a functional atheist. I believed, yes, but only as a mental Christian. I professed what I was supposed to believe, but my living was hardly distinguishable from that of the nice nonbeliever.

Painfully I remember being invited to deliver a lecture on "God" to a national conference. Never once did it occur to me to pray for guidance in preparation, or even to give thanks to God for the standing ovation. I had done it all myself, thank you! But on the flight back home I knew. Regardless of what I might say to the contrary, the silent witness of my life at that time was that God is dead.

Likewise, during much of my life, religious practices have been an embarrassment, whether I did them, or whether I did not—either way. Had persons confided in me that they had not been intimate with their spouse for months, I would know that the marriage was in trouble. Analogously, then, what if I were asked how long it had been since I had been intimate with God? I would have to confess: "Never!" That's right, never! And me a theologian!

It has taken me far too long to recognize the trouble. I was teaching what I did not live, living what I did not acknowledge, and being oblivious to the difference. My life had moments of ecstasy, to be sure—musically, sexually, and at daybreak. But *by what right can I think that my loss of self in Bach's* Concerto for Two Violins in D Minor *is an experience of God?*

As I ponder here in my hermitage, things are becoming clearer. As deeply as I can ascertain, I set aside last year for the hermit experience because I was determined to "have it out." I wanted to undergo serious spiritual practice, and subsequently be brought to the crossroad. Then I would know—either by being brought to discover God, or to know myself as an honest atheist who would leave seminary teaching.

Sitting by the lake today, watching a great blue heron gulp a noonday snack, I remember how difficult my first three-month monastic experience was seven years ago in Colorado. I had to fight the temptation endemic to all academicians. I was tempted to spend my sabbatical in the Harvard library writing a book on prayer, thereby escaping totally the need to pray. That is why I placed myself during those months in a position where I could not escape the confrontation. I would be immersed in a monastery where even carrots are peeled to the glory of God. During the intervening years, much of the initial experience has been lost. But what has prevailed is the effect of being bitten by the silence. As I am an extrovert, how can it be that silence is becoming downright delicious? There is something authentic about it, for it becomes an internal process of being stripped of the noise that culture designs to insulate us from ourselves. And it was such silencing, step-by-step, peeling after peeling, which claimed me. I did not identify that as God—not yet. What claimed me at heart level was the unavoidableness of the God question.

Saturday, June 6

These are distinctive days. I have the time to do nothing else but permit my self to be swept clean by the Spirit. At daybreak, I offer the day to God, promising to be open to whatever vulnerability God might choose for me. After several hours of simple pondering, I can say that last year I actually made a step toward the outer edge of faith. Karl Rahner's challenge to me is deceptively simple. I am to trust that the craving for God in my soul is the primal evidence of the existence of the God who is seeking me. In my reading this morning, Merton's way of putting it makes the connection that I need. While we may feel nothing but God's absence, the mere fact that we seek God proves that God has already found us.

Can I trust that? Yes, but maybe not. No, but maybe so. I suspect that this is the deepest reason for why I felt so strongly the need to be immersed in the silence—to plunge in, all the way, to see if I could trust. I desperately want to believe, to believe that God is the rightful name for the cause of my having been burned with a brand-shaped WHY. Yes, questions upon questions. And yet I must say it again: What claimed me during those original monastic three months in Colorado is the immersion in a community that is centered daily around the altar. "Sacred" is the unavoidable word, where we lift bread and wine as far as the human arms can stretch, rivaled only by the mystery of the early fog descending into the chalice of the surrounding mountains. During such moments, and in that place, God does "exist." Yes. But I left.

I should not be surprised by how soon the old rhythms reemerge. It is not the noise of TV that does me in. I refuse to own one. Is it the night sounds of sirens, drunks, breaking glass? No. It is the days. How quickly I permit them to become jammed full with teaching, counseling, and administration. I even avoid seminary chapel in order to flee from more talk. I am consumed by doing. *That is it. Consumed! Driven! That is why I reentered the monastic life last year. There, I have said it!*

The importance of those first monastic months during the summer of 1971, then, might well be the role they were to play in the slowly emerging crisis that came to a head in 1986–87, the period I am now struggling to understand. For this second immersion, I chose to be at the Trappist monastery in the Ozark Mountains. Because it is so much closer to home, I could be more certain that its proximity would haunt me from then on. I entered that monastery for several months of intense preparation in order to undergo an extended hermit experience for the rest of the nine-month sabbatical. But with more than an edge of self-anger, I must now honestly make this confession: I was forced to return to the monastery after only a very short time in the hermitage, and for one crucial reason. I failed. It is not that I was insufficiently informed about the hermit life. Not at all. I know now what it was. In the lonely hours there is no denying one fact. Whatever I thought I was battling outside of me took up residency deeply within me. It is I who is driven to fill the emptiness inside with intense doing outside. Simply put, I am a living self-contradiction. I choose to live in an inner city ghetto out of conscience, yet I yearn for silence. And when I find

silence on weekends in my hermitage, I turn on news broad-
casts and yearn for the world. "Purity of heart," said Soren
Kierkegaard, "is to will one thing." I could not. I simply could
not. Even my drivenness fails to have a disciplined focus.

My teaching colleagues are no help. They are as driven as
I. They, too, refuse to take a day off, are unwilling to take a
vacation, and pridefully plan their tired schedules several years
in advance. They intimidate me. What a cruel way of ending
my day. A persistent whippoorwill is my solace.

Sunday, June 7

I rise early, for by the time the morning light begins, my
thinking is already in high gear. With coffee, pencil, and paper,
in that order, I let my rambling mind turn over whatever stones
it comes upon. The first is an acknowledgement that there is at
least a modicum of honesty in last year's endeavor. I had the
courage to begin what could well have been my final year as a
professor. At stake is whether in good conscience I can any
longer prepare persons for Christian ministry. Even more: Are
my own Christian roots so soggy that they can no longer pretend
to provide a personal foundation? It is not long until I understand
that the desert is the name for walking into one's weakness. It is
the landscape with shadows. Thus, as an extrovert, my weakness
is silence, underscored by loneliness. Hagar, Moses, Rahab,
Jeremiah, John, and Jesus—each had their own desert to enter,
alone. I was to be next.

I suspected, then, with fear, that what the desert will
require of me is to relinquish my patent rights on the Protestant

work ethic. How? By discovering why I am so addicted. Even so, little do I suspect at the beginning that this will entail a total upheaval of my life. More than I ever realized, doing is the only thing holding together the pieces that purport to be me. Thus it brings fear even to suspect that my doing will be the first thing for me to renounce.

Saturday, June 13

During this past week, mornings no longer have been a cherished time. The notes and entries and anything else that could serve as reminders of my hermit months remain in semi-neat piles. They have the same suggested labels that I gave them a week or so ago, when I first tried to bring order out of the past year. I have not touched any of this since. Clearly I am not yet ready either to refine further the piles with additional sorting, or to begin working my way though even one of these piles.

Avoidance, no doubt. But on the positive side, I might be right in providing more time just to ponder, letting the aroma of the year pass in and out of my mind. I chuckle over an image that emerges, almost like a koan for meditation. Here I am, struggling to be a serious Christian in the twentieth century by following dutifully someone who is a product of his own time twenty centuries ago. I picture how silly, if not disastrous, it would be for Jesus to address the yearly stockholder meetings of corporate America. He would advise them, no doubt, not to be anxious about their life—about eating, drinking, clothing, or even the adequacy of insurance coverage or medical copayments. Life, he would insist, is to be lived not for the sake of reputation or financial compensation, but for the sheer daily joy of living life as a child of God. Then would come his proposal: Give away your stock which is linked to tomorrow, for the sake of the fullness of living one day at a time. And if today is too big a chunk as a start, learn from the sparrows to flutter fully with life in each moment. I imagine he would receive no standing ovation. I wonder what he would wear. Jesus in a tuxedo—that is worth pondering.

I may be making fun, but only to divert my nervousness. The content of such a Jesus speech is precisely what has worked itself into my insides—not so much as an invitation, but as an imperative. The saints provide multiple models for taking Jesus' words to heart. But most of all it is the ruthless precision of Jesus' own desert experience that haunts me. How can he get from being a shy local carpenter who did not impress anyone, to exuding a charisma that has changed the world? The answer is that he takes the path leading through the center of the desert. He lives thirty silent, hidden years, outwardly working with wood, but inwardly roaming the hills and feeling his times and discovering the yearnings of his soul. Then he makes his wager. And as he is baptized, "the heaven was opened, and the Holy Spirit descended upon him" (Luke 3:21-22). And immediately the Spirit who had taken up residency in him led him into the desert where he lived as a hermit for forty days and forty nights (Luke 4:1f.). There he is skillfully tempted. This is for real, because Scripture would never call them temptations unless Jesus is indeed battling his own cravings for prestige, power, and possessions. Today, however, the situation is far worse. In his time these temptations were widely acknowledged as immoral, giving societal support for resisting them. But in our times, not only are these ingredients not perceived as temptations, as something to be overcome, but have become goals to be attained. So much is this so that society rewards those who forcefully play by the competitive rules that function as the cornerstone of American society. And here I am, a poverty kid who made good, shaped by society into being a Horatio Alger whose success apparently proves the American Dream to be a reliable promise—ready to give it all up. Incredible, for I had it all, and then, intentionally, enter the desert to give it all away.

Yet it is not quite that simple. In the desert I discover how impossible this relinquishing is, by human effort. The three desert temptations do not just come to me from the outside, in regard to which I am free either to accept or reject. They are me. I have been forged and shaped and injected with them since birth. Both school and society teach me to use them as the measure of success in being a human being. Yes, the deep interior pulsation that impels me is precisely the drive to be through doing. And how does it feel to live in such a fashion? The feeling is complex, but some of its primal ingredients are the ongoing sense of never being able to do enough, of being persistently anxious about not succeeding, of hiding from others who I really am, of trying to prove something that does not have a name, and having to start all over again each morning.

There are times in the desert when I believe that nothing less than exorcism can free me. And to make things even more confused, I wrestle over not only doubting that I have sufficient courage to change, but also that I cannot even muster the desire to want to change. The reward for succumbing to these temptations has served me well. Appalachia is five states away, and the road out of it has been paved for me. I should have known, but I did not, how serious the desert surgery would be.

Tuesday, June 16

On the deck, as I enjoy the filtered greenness of the morning sun, I acknowledge that the internal logic with which I lived as I entered my hermit time made sense, in a sick sort of way. It is fairly simple and straightforward. If by the quantity of my doing I can convince others that I am worthwhile, then I should be able to accept myself as having worth. Actually it did work, sometimes—for a while. But now, in the twilight of my life's journey, I discover as a hermit that the driving issue is no longer simply the need to prove myself to others. The situation is much worse. This drivenness has become such an integral part of me that I cannot imagine myself capable of living with me without it.

Thursday, June 18

Having acknowledged how bound by doing I have been for most of my life, I am making an effort today just to be. Yet by midmorning prayer time, I cannot quiet the dilemma I confessed last year just as I was ready to take my step into the desert. It has to do with doing—it seems that it always does. The payment always extracted from me for taking any time off is guilt. Related to that, I confess that I have never known myself to be happy. The closest I have come is ending any day with sufficient fatigue to justify sleep as a reward for well doing. Yet I have to acknowledge that even after a night of "rewarded" sleep, the process begins all over again by morning. The achievement slate gets mysteriously wiped clean each night. By Vesper time, I am quite aware that this theme was at the heart of my conversion last year—and now, hopefully, it will become an active dynamic more than a puzzling memory.

Sunday, June 21

I am spending too much time inside the hermitage. Feeling captive to my day-after-day thinking, I hike to the cliffs overlooking the lake. Yet even in the midst of such serene beauty, I am unable to let go. In part, this is because of what happened last year. It opened in me a willingness to be emotionally vulnerable. In being stripped of the ordinary defense mechanisms I had been building all my life, for the first time deep feelings were permitted to flow in and out. And even though this is happening today with frightening rapidity, I recognize that I am still hesitant, at times even defensive, about letting my feelings run free again. The resistance I am feeling is no less than a hesitancy to let happen what I know I must. I know what happened last year, but I do not know yet how to feel about it. *Yes, that is it. As a heavy thinker, according to the Myers-Briggs scales, my inevitable shadow is the opposite, which is feeling. As they are the least developed, often I am not even in touch with them. An important part of my learning in the desert is to recognize how elaborate, even skillful, are the intellectual defenses I erect to keep my feelings out of the way. No wonder that this past month has been such an intense time of thinking. I have reverted. Yes, but down deep I acknowledge that these defenses have become tottery. They will not be able to postpone much longer my dealing with my deep feelings. They are so close to the surface that I fear they will erupt at any moment. Even so, I cannot deny that my shadow still possesses some power to haunt me.*

I am not sure how long I sat on the cliffs, but it was long enough to acknowledge the primal feeling that gnawed at me, sending me on last year's pilgrimage. Most of my life I have felt as if I was born in arrears, with my birth certificate doubling as a mortgage agreement against my name. And although I could never live long enough to pay it off, to renege on any payments would be like having my forehead marked with a red stamp reading "Failure." Nathaniel Hawthorne's Hester in The Scarlet Letter was required to wear a huge red "A," so that all would know of her adultery. On the edge of the desert last year, I was certain that I would be made to wear a red "F."

Monks order their lives with seven Daily Offices. When I was living in the city, however, I ordered mine with a perennial list of things needing to be done. "To do nothing and feel no guilt," Merton once said, is "the beginning of spirituality." Precisely, and in the city I was brought to an overwhelming awareness: I could not even meet the entrance requirements.

Sunday, July 5

Yesterday's clarity began today with embarrassment. I still remember the day when I discovered with delight in one of Merton's books a confession that meant that I was not alone in the vicious-circle version of living. How better to have Merton as one's company in sin? This is the key sentence: "I am a contemplative who is ready to collapse from overwork." Can Catholics die of the Protestant work ethic? He then describes quite well the desert experience toward which both he and I are being pushed. He indicates that the desert's beginning will no doubt entail being "stripped of one illusion after another." For what purpose? To be brought face to face with the question that neither he nor I could long avoid. This is his guess as to what his primal desert question would turn out to be: "Why I read so much, why I write so much, why I talk so much, and why I get so excited about the things that only affect the surface of my life." Yes, that is my hunch, too.

His lament touches deeply the pathos that I have known for so long. "I am worn out with activity," he exclaims, "exhausting myself with proclaiming that the thing to do is rest." One of his sentences is particularly lethal when he identifies by name the "desert walk" that he and I need to take. "In order to be not remembered or even wanted, I have to be content to become a person that nobody knows." These are the seeds that finally sprout for Merton into the craving for a hermitage. And yet, when he is finally given permission to enter one, the sideshow going on inside his head will not let him stay. A model for me he is not—for he, too, fought for and against the desert until his death, apparently without ever having come out whole on the other side.

With Merton as an accomplice in spiritual confusion, I finally risk sorting through a particularly tattered pile of my journal, intent on finding my entry thoughts. What I found I seemed to know by heart:

"I need to be a hermit because I need to go where no one will see, or know, or care. I need to do nothing that could possibly justify my year, or me, or life, or anything. Then I will be forced just to be—for its own sake. Or . . . or . . . that is what terrifies me."

That is it precisely. My need is to become clear with myself.

Months before I began this hermit plunge, I shared my plan with a friend. His response seemed reasonable: "Why mess around with the monastery bit. Just go to your hermitage and do it!" For three days this made sense, as I prepared to cancel my monastery arrangement. Then, with unexpected anger, I called him. "I'm shocked that I let you talk me out of the monastery." "But you've experienced monasteries before. Why do that trip again?" I blurted it out: "Because I need permission to do nothing!" I was shocked by my own words. They were true.

How prophetic they proved to be during my first month at the monastery. I kept being pressed into awareness of this weakness—of needing permission to do the obvious. Yet I can see now that far more was needed, and it is this need that accounts for what eventually went wrong. How clear it is now. What I

*am really seeking necessitates nothing less than a conversion,
followed by an intense formation in living "as if." Musicians
need the serious discipline of rehearsing over and over again;
otherwise it is the musician, not Bach, who is heard at the
concert. This is what the several months of preparation at the
monastery were to be, but they proved to be insufficient formation for enduring the long and treacherous hermit aloneness.*

Tuesday, July 7

My monastic preparation began quite seriously, a year
ago last May. The reading assignments I was given focus on
the early desert hermits. I find myself quickly identifying with
these fourth-century anchorites, for their motivation helps me
see more clearly why I am doing what I am trying to do. They
and I are uttering a physical no to each of our cultural situations. Beginning in the fourth century, Christians are no
longer persecuted. Instead, Christianity becomes acceptable,
even advantageous. As a result, the desert experience begins
to replace martyrdom as the mark of the serious Christian.
Seen from this perspective, Christians who permit themselves
to be shaped by secular culture are guilty not only of betraying
God but of losing their own true selves. The hermits call this
madness, for it means attachment to unreal values. The
more I read, the more I am convinced that their situation
parallels closely my own. The hermit's task, both then and
now, is to purge this false self of its societal and personal pre-
occupations, until the distinction between living and praying
disappears.

Through my reading I come to regard "desert" as the name for any exterior environment sufficient to evoke a purification of the desert within. The desert experience occurs, then, when delusions are so burned away through loneliness that the true self can respond to the invitation to emerge. And as this happens, the silence that is so threatening becomes a garment of healing. To follow Christ heroically into the inner solitude requires first the daring to enter into a physical isolation. Because hermits are willing, they become the unrecognized explorers on behalf of us all, probing life at its deepest and outer edges. In so doing, they are living guides, functioning as invitation and promise to the rest of humankind.

Thursday, July 9

I just came from a noontime walk by the lake. This is my daily time for doing lectio divina, *as monks call it. The method is to read and reread a passage of Scripture until I feel so addressed that I am invited into meditation. Today it takes only several verses for my mind to recall appreciatively how last year the desert image as a major theme gave coherence and new life to the Bible as a whole. This theme of the desert is central to the Old Testament. On the positive side we have Israel's cathartic desert wanderings. On the negative side we have Israel's exile purgation. It is intriguing that when the vision lures them from the desert into the Promised Land, only in looking back do they recognize the hard forty desert years as their honeymoon with God. And when, in turn, they forget their desert experience, tragedy inevitably awaits. When they* no longer know themselves as rooted in the desert, the illusion of self-sufficiency flourishes, and their love affair with God is dissipated into a marriage of inconvenience. I come to understand Israel painfully through my own desert experience. Every time that by frenzied "doing" they and I gain the fat of plenty and the arrogance of success, a hard exile in the desert awaits us. Only through the desert that is without were they, and I, able to find healing for the corrosive desert within. Last year I learned the hard way that the dynamic of Israel's history is the necessary rhythm each Christian must experience.

Sunday, July 12

My Scripture reading today continues my meditation from yesterday. Looking back on those preparatory months with the perspective of hindsight, it is significant how much my Christology is changing. In my youth, "Jesus talk" embarrassed me, for my friends and I had the image of someone meek and mild, a pushover and a wimp. But in the desert, Jesus becomes for me a hero figure. He is the one who succeeds where Israel fails—continuously. His life is the desert experience—thirty concealed years, forty days of wilderness temptation, countless night vigils in the lonely mountains, a face set steadfastly toward a Jerusalem death, the bloody sweat on the Mount of Olives, the Gethsemane betrayal, his torture through scourging, his unbelievable suffering by crucifixion, death among outcasts on a hill called "the Skull," and his final cry of dereliction. And in the hermitage silence I come to recognize this hero Christ as silhouette for the serious Christian. The bottom line to which I come is this: Without the Christ event, I would be an atheist. Everything depends on faith as this wager: that in Jesus as the Christ, the very character and intention of God for the cosmos is disclosed. For me it has come down to this. It is Jesus, or not at all.

Wednesday, July 15

Today I become aware of the significant part that reading about the eremitic life played during my months of monastic formation. But perhaps even more important is the fact that at the monastery I have hermits all around me who serve as models. I just found the journal page in which I described how blessed I was.

"I marvel at what a rich environment this monastery is proving to be as preparation for hermit living. Where else could one find an abbot who was a personal friend of Thomas Merton, and was one of the first Trappists after Merton to receive permission to be a hermit? There is another hermit here whose hermitage is close to the monastery, who came here through the peace movement to Zen. In addition there are two hermitages on monastic land serving as invitations for each monk to become hermits for short times on a regular basis. In addition, there is another hermitage in which lives a full-time hermit, who is the ex-abbot and my spiritual director. There is also a community of six women hermits two miles away, with a hermit monk as chaplain. As if this is not enough, there is a hermit family down the road—a husband, wife, and three children. They were given permission to build a homestead on *monastic land, make a living through selling herbs, home school their children, and worship with the monks."*

In my varied conversations with all these hermits, their gentle manner of sharing keeps bringing me back to the theme that serves as their center—grace as unconditional love. This alone, they insist, is able to penetrate so deeply that the diseased soul finds healing in the desert. All of them begin at the same place, acknowledging themselves as being unacceptable. Then each of them comes to the same resolution: trusting that God totally accepts us—always as a nevertheless, *and never as a* because.

Thus I have not only stories of the ancient hermits, but also access to the stories of the hermits who surround me with their presence.

I remember especially the first story told me by one of the hermits about his desert experience. His description turned out to be representative of most hermits I was to meet. "In my first hermitage," he confessed, "the feeling that I had lost everything terrified me. My brothers in the monastery had given up everything too, but at least they had each other. I was utterly alone. Yet it was in this desperate sense of nothingness that I began to sense a nevertheless, *an acceptance, a "Oneness." Then came my illumination. Everything in each moment rests for its existence on the grounding power of Being, as Life itself, closer than I am to myself. I have little use for concepts. They are limits. My concern is with the Limitlessness at the Center, as the inside of everything. I would guess that you too will be able to distill your desert experience in these three words: emptiness, acceptance, and embrace."*

His hermitage is typical of most of the others I would visit. It has a kitchen corner, table, bed, icon, desk, and a chair by a window overlooking the hills.

Sunday, July 19

My remembrances yesterday of the hermits whose lives surround me left out probably the most important influence. The community of women hermits especially becomes my formative image. This is the way my journal described the community and my first visit.

"Bethany Community is at the end of a winding logging road, straddling a high ridge. In the center of a small clearing is a low-slung chapel, hugging the earth. It appears to be made of stones, but they are actually rejects from the monastic block factory. A belfry holds the doorbell, with a chain that invites the visitor to ring it. I did. With a touch of mystery, the chaplain emerged from the woods. In his long personal pilgrimage he has been a novice master, has led an expansion community, and is a trained Scripture scholar, a lover of the patristics, a priest, and the designer and primary builder of this community. He is friendly, articulate, committed, and a fine listener. His presence makes clear that a hermit is not a recluse. 'A hermit,' he volunteered, 'is called of God to a special vocation of prayer, not to be an eccentric personality.'

The chapel, with solar windows to the south, has benches on three sides with kneeling cushions, comfortably designed for perhaps ten persons. Simplicity and silence are the unifying themes, centered in the stone altar. Connected to this chapel is *a pleasant kitchen/dining area with bookcases. Here the community does its planning at the one weekly common meal. The other communal building is a combination laundry, canning room, root cellar, and greenhouse. A large garden supplies most of their needs—stored, frozen, and canned. Each hermit simply comes and takes whatever food she needs. This food supply is supplemented by occasional visits to town in a pickup truck.*

Seven hermitages are scattered throughout the trees, on both sides of the ridge. Each is slightly different, as experience leads to increased efficiency of design. The newer ones are cut into the southern hillside, with passive solar heating supplemented by a wood stove. There is electricity, well water, indoor plumbing, but no telephone. Each one-room interior has the same functional areas—a chapel, workspace, desk, kitchen, bath, bed, and window vista. The bed and chapel area are always adjacent.

This community is self-sustained. While a small foundation grant helped in the beginning, they have never been in debt. Income comes through crafts and a part-time proofreading job. They are clear as to what they are about—contemplation. Eucharist is their only daily gathering. In the summer, the work is primarily gardening, and in the fall, food storage. The winter, I was told, is a hibernation in the Spirit, 'a time of special silence and warm contentment.'

These hermits are strikingly friendly, gentle, and happy, living from the inside out. I asked what the daily life in their hermitages was like. 'The monastic schedule of seven daily offices helps to fall back on, but I listen to my body in determining the daily rhythm, and I watch the flow of the seasons.

*Winter is the most quiet and prayerful.' 'Is it difficult?' 'Yes,
very. Without God this life would be unbearable. But with
God as center there is an inner quiet and joy.' 'Do you have
common ingredients to your separateness?' 'Usually we all
do* lectio divina *(sacred reading), contemplation, daily
offices, manual labor, study, the Eucharist together—and
most of us like nature. To the extent that our prayer life is
pure, our intercessions pour out for the whole world.' 'What
more can one ask?' 'Nothing.' Such gentle integrity is rare.
Is it enough?"*

As a person whose days are always structured by a list of
things needing to be done, it is difficult for me at that time to
picture what their days of "being" would be like. It does not take
long for me to find out. My assigned spiritual director turns out
to be a hermit, too. "Being" is his total way of living.
Therefore, beginning with our first session, I push him hard to
find out what such a life is really like.

"I asked my spiritual director to describe his day as a hermit. He rises at 1:30 AM with a short prayer of thanksgiving.
After dressing in the dark, he does the liturgy of Vigils, as at the
monastery. A simple breakfast follows, perhaps an apple with
coffee. Then, until dawn, he sits in darkness, facing the tabernacle in the wall over his bed. His sole intent is to be 'aware of
the Presence.' 'But what if you don't experience it?' 'Then I do
scriptural meditation, or simply remember that God loves me
anyhow. It's okay, no matter what happens.'

At dawn, he does Lauds, followed by the Eucharist,
paralleling again the monastic rhythm. 'I have a period of special

thanksgiving after communion. Through the elements, the God I seek becomes incarnated in me.' So prepared, he feels ready to read Scripture, slowly, repetitively. At midmorning, he does the office of Terce, followed by work—repairs, cutting wood, washing dishes. His main meal at noon consists of bread, cheese, and fruit, followed by the short office of Sext. At 3 PM two days of the week, he goes to the monastery and does book-keeping, laundry, or clothing repair. *'Then I return to the hermitage, pick off the ticks, read Scripture, eat a simple snack, and do Compline—in that order!'* His day ends much as it begins—sitting in the Presence, until sleep becomes a force to be acknowledged, usually around 7 PM. *'Why this particular schedule?' 'Because the night hours are the most sacred.'*

I am struck by the happiness of this man. Although old by cultural standards, his aura is that of a young boy—gentle, excited, in love with life in the living of it. Have I ever met a happy person before? I know some who may be content, even a few who appreciate life. But happy? I personally discarded that word long ago as useless. Yet here he is, happily defying our cultural measures for comfort and success. His one-room, tarpaper shack, perched on a high hill, has no electricity, refrigeration, or running water. There is a single propane burner for cooking, a potbellied stove for heat, and a cistern filled by roof runoff for bathing."

Can holiness mean to live wholly? I have never before known anyone this free. "That is what the desert is about," he tries to explain. "All I want is to grow old loving my God."

This is the man, as my spiritual director, who will haunt me from this first visit to the present. One of his many gifts is teaching me how to contemplate, or the prayer of centering, as some call it. For him it is a way of being. The method is to repeat a word or phase over and over again to keep my thinking out of the way, until I am wooed into silence—and everything is stillness. This practice comes hard for me. I resist it. Yet, in spite of my drivenness to keep doing, doing anything, doing everything, one fine evening at the monastery it finally comes.

"I have been trying for a month now to sense what monastic prayer life might be like. So as I did daily work with various monks, I invited them to share their experience with prayer. I heard three themes repeatedly. 'It is God who gives the desire and hunger for prayer; so if you have this, it is simply a matter of setting times aside to let it happen.' 'Contemplation is that unique, honest time, wherein I give all I have, which is my nothingness. Such nakedness becomes a Divine nearness.' And third, 'The heart of Spirit life is a deep quiet in which by repeating a word such as "God," one becomes content simply in being.'

In turn, I asked for personal feedback from these monks as hints for my own spiritual maturity. Their suggestions formed two common themes: 'Talk less' and 'Drink deeply of the Silence.' My spiritual director agreed, saying that everything depends upon contemplation as 'going into the silence.' 'Just go to the chapel and be.' 'What should I do?' 'Nothing!' I pushed frantically for elaboration. 'Just stop whatever you are doing. Whatever. Everything. Stop!' It occurred to me later that maybe what he wanted me to do was stop!

And so this evening after Compline I return to the chapel for a period of 'nothingness.' 'Let go,' he had said. The sun is setting behind the stained-glass windows. It is a warm evening.

The gentle summer sounds wash in through an open window.
Peace. I settle in, deliberately devoid of thinking. I am just here.
'It' is here. 'We' are here? Being? Is this what it's all about?
Presence? So simple. This is as much peace as I have ever
known. I could stay here. When it is time to leave, whatever
that means, I thank the growing Darkness, and bow toward the
candle of Presence.

I leave the chapel, finding myself walking on tiptoe so as
not to disturb a sleeping world. Interestingly, I observe that I
am no longer striding down the center of the cloister. I am simply
gliding along at its edge. And from my bed, I watch clouds out
the window. There seems no need to chase them any more. My
bed is warm and light. I feel mellow and content—and healing.
By the time the moon comes up, I am sensing from within that
contemplation is to experience myself as grounded in, and with,
and as, and for all that is. I feel remorse for anyone whom I
have ever hurt; and compassion for everything that is hurting. I
need no longer to compete with anyone. All that I want, I
am—and I wish nothing less for every person. Rather than
being centered by doing, life is becoming a matter of not standing
in the way. The night sounds become my mantra. I will sleep
very well tonight."

Tuesday, July 21

Today I remembered a related special time, and found it
in my journal.

"*After Compline, the whole monastery settles into the*
Great Silence, as the nightly foretaste of death. I return to the

chapel for contemplation. But some retreatants are holding a conversation outside the window. As the noise stretches on, I feel as if I am gulping for silence. One by one they leave. I descend into the stillness. Strangely, the deeper it becomes, the more accessible become the distant sounds—a chain saw far across the valley, a cow over some distant hill, a bird nestling in nearby. They wash over me, a kind of forest surf, until separate noises blend into the musical sound called night. It is tangible—the silence and the slow dancing."

Such times are blessed, as undeserved gifts. And I find that the more I am able to sense what being is all about, the more my passion for social justice makes guest appearances. While these two will continue to struggle with each other throughout the desert time, I am given an early insight that has lasting significance for this struggle.

"I just read a pamphlet written by some representatives of feminine monasticism. Their concern is to weld together contemplation and social justice. In a world where fifteen thousand persons starve to death daily, they insist that what is needed is a vision of both structural and personal reform. The monastery is rooted in such a vision, prophetically living and offering its extended family community as a model for the world.

If this is so, I tell myself, then this monastery hidden in the back folds of the Ozark hills is really an interlocking village. It is where tithing for the 'sojourner, the fatherless, and the widow' is a global witness that all extremes of poverty and affluence must be outlawed. The monastic call is a voluntary identification with the poor, the voiceless, and the marginal.

And its answer? *A life of simplicity and moderation, in which even the humblest objects receive respect as if, said Saint Benedict, they are 'vessels of the altar.'*

This is the first time that I have experienced the prophetic as having such gentle, spiritual roots. Recognizing the face of Christ in each stranger is the personal formula for healing. And the structural counterpart is that of seeing the world monastically, in which common ownership is the primary right. If the goods of the earth belong to God, then we are stewards rather than owners, called to see that they are used equally by and for all. 'Monastic economics' is revolutionary, calling for a conversion of 'materialism, consumerism, and overconsumption'—so that no one is left outside the cosmic hospitality."

Thursday, July 23

Over a breakfast of eggs, toast, and writing paper, I feel ready to put into words what the preparatory months last year taught me. The result is like a collage, intertwining intellectual encounters with new ideas, hearing invitations into an alternative way of life, and being exposed to strong role models. With all this, I can see why I thought I was ready to live in my own hermitage. I was wrong. How gaping is the chasm between knowing the map and hiking the trail. I just found the journal entry that turned out to be prophetic.

"For my siesta after lunch, I curl up with a study of priests and their problems with prayer. With the first paragraph, it becomes clear that the reason for my being here is widespread. 'In order to pray, one must first be healed of the fear of being

alone.' Yes. And to enjoy being alone, one 'must have a strong, positive self image.' Yes again. 'This', the study concludes, 'is what a large number of priests do not have, with our culture accentuating the dilemma. Solitude has so little value for modern society that we are made to feel that something is wrong with us if we are alone.' The conclusion that was drawn from this widespread condition touched me directly. Unfortunately, unless priests find some benefit from praying, they apparently have no interest in doing it, and thus do not. Prayer needs to be for its own sake.

This is certainly an accurate portrait of me, but I am stunned that it is so widespread among the clergy. Even though pastors are supposed to be models for a life of prayer, the power of 'doing' over 'being' is as deadly within them as it is within me. While I am beginning to sense how wrong this is, I nonetheless share with my fellow pastors that fatal criterion: that unless spirituality, and even God, can be seen to be 'useful,' it has no meaning. But this is an absurd stance, for it reduces all things spiritual to being simply a means for some nonspiritual end that is valued more highly. This is the riddle I cannot yet break. But I have a hunch it has something to do with the fact that 'doing' always requires a reward for doing.

I am beginning to sense how much healing it will take simply to aim me in the right direction—back to a Calvin for whom the primary end of life is to 'glorify God and enjoy God forever.' What is at stake here seems to have little to do with either getting or giving. An analogy is helping me to make sense of this quandary. For a relationship with someone to be deep, it *must be for its own sake. It must have about it a lyric delight. To use that friendship for some other end would be to poison it, rendering it quite grim. I have a hunch that my relationship with God, if it exists, is of the grim kind.*

Perhaps the most severe warning of what might be ahead came early in my final month of preparation. I begin to see how much agreement there seems to be between the spirituality of the desert saints and therapy. Both seem to be saying to me in a troubling way that the root of my problem is my 'will to live'. But that is the very thing I most admire about myself: the assertive energy to take on almost anything. Yet I should not need will power to do what I really want to do. But I do. So does that mean, at a deeper level, that I really want to die? I am frightened. Living is hard work! I have difficulty getting out of bed each morning. It does take will power just to begin living again every day. I want to roll over and fade out of existence. Only when guilt finally cuts in can I get up. Then all day I struggle to bury my feelings, for it is easier to will to live if I do not feel.

It is confession time. I confess that I want to die. Life is too much, always trying to measure up, performing, balancing the ledger, trying to make myself worthwhile. I'm tired of it. I've paid my dues, damn it! I want to turn life off, at least for a while. Let me be! But to whom am I yelling? That is the question. So here I am, holding on for dear life to the same frantic pace—because letting go would be suicide. I strongly suspect, and fear, that my desert experience will entail the need to provide for my plot the missing names, faces, and places. I am almost as terrified to do it, as I am afraid that it might not happen."

Yes, terrified. I am able to acknowledge now, after the fact, that this is indeed the correct word. Fortunately I did not know at the time just how frightening the desert experience would be. If I had, I probably would have run for my life in the opposite direction, only to ruin what life I have left with a new version of the game called "Avoidance."

Sunday, July 26

Even after three months at the monastery, I did not suspect what was ahead. But the next day I left for my desert, driving unsuspectingly to my hermitage, right on schedule. My noble but naïve intent was to test that strangeness called Christianity, walking into its silence with only my weaknesses as luggage. My spiritual director might have had more of a premonition than I, for he proposed that I try living in my hermitage for ten days, and then return for a final three weeks in the monastery. This sounded reasonable. What could go wrong in ten days?

My hermitage experience gets off to a good start. This is the way I recorded it.

"After Vigils at the monastery (3:30 AM) and with a cup of coffee for the road, I was on my way to the hermitage. It is so fine to be loved. One of the monks left a freshly baked loaf of bread at my cell door, with a note: 'Come back soon. We will pray for you at your hermitage. And in a special way at each Eucharist we will be sharing lives, even at a distance.' I will be almost three hours away. There were quiet hugs. I drove down *the road toward a freshly cut sliver of moon. In the shadows along the highway a monk was jogging by starlight. I caught his wave in the rear-view mirror."*

Yet even with such a sendoff, this first day of my ten days at my hermitage witnesses a rapid return to my deadly pattern.

"I had difficulty not speed-reading Lauds. I had to say each word deliberately out loud. Even so, it was like a race to get it done. 'A waste of time' was the thought that kept rising from the dead. This has been my lifelong refrain, and here it is, beginning before I have even started. If I were doing Lauds with the monks, that would be one thing. But here, all alone, it suddenly makes no sense. It is like talking to myself! I got through it by getting it done. Then I filled the silence with music. For the first time in weeks, I had sexual feelings. As the day moved on, I found myself resisting the scheduled monastic liturgy. I had intended to do all the offices, exactly when and how they were being done at the monastery. At this very moment, the breviary is in front of me. I cannot bring myself to pick up the book and do even one of them."

A journal entry indicates that the evening is no better.

"It is late now, and I am finally going to bed, more out of fatigue than intention. It is like the bad 'good old times.' I need closure for the day. I can't find it, probably because I don't think I have done anything worth closing! I opened a book of prayers and picked one: 'God, may I be in your presence, even though I know it only as absence.' That will have to do. Amen."

Monday, July 27

Today I dared to read more from my journal regarding that first self-encounter at my hermitage.

"Perhaps this was my worst day in a long while. What a terrible day! Could it be worse? I slept late. I awoke to a weird combination of guilt and defiance. I'm lonely. I crave news, any news. So I devoured two old newspapers saved for starting fires. One article, tucked away on page 36, revealed that 47 percent of black teenagers are unemployed. That didn't help a bit."

I tried an unopened letter. It is from a friend.

How was your time at the monastery? Did you shed yourself of the world's and your own troubles for a time, and release yourself to God's gentleness? Or did you continue to wage wars? I have been haunted by your words when last I saw you. "Sometimes life gets to be too much." They were combined with a trapped look in your eyes and a desperate note in your voice. Why are you so sad, deep inside? Perhaps the better question is, what are you really seeking? I pray that you find it.

Terrific! Not at all what I need to hear.

"I have been working constantly since I arrived at the hermitage, clearing the clutter, doing the doing, and feeling guilty for not doing more. I feel like Sisyphus, always pushing something up the hill to create space in order to create space in order to create space. Why? I am simply powerless to give *myself permission to be. That's it. I peck away at life's piles from all angles, hoping that by working harder I can devour them faster. But all that this seems to do is to encourage their spontaneous generation. I think of my spiritual director, in his tarpaper shack with no running water and little insulation, in a hot field where chiggers and ticks scrimmage daily. And he's happy! God, I hope so."*

My remaining days at the hermitage creep by, so very slowly, all much the same—lacking in enthusiasm, direction, will power, and purpose. My final day is an important day of reckoning:

"This morning I got up exhausted, almost aching. I did the chores that needed to be done. Then I gave up and took a nap. This dynamic went on most of the day, fighting it, and then giving up. It ended up with me sleeping too much.

Clearly my preparatory period at the monastery was as mandatory as it was insufficient. Wisely my spiritual director had insisted that I return. Any authority residing in the interaction between my desires and my will seems able to last just about as long as the ride from the monastery to the hermitage. If I really want to escape my work-drivenness, then why do reported successes by my friends threaten me so? I confess that last week I was depressed for a full day after hearing that one of my colleagues had a manuscript accepted for publication. Without the desert purgation, what I am about will be nothing more than 'sour grapes' brought on by aging.

Before returning to the monastery, I need honesty. Have I learned anything? For hours I sat. I thought. I wrote. Such loneliness. *I was born alone and I will die alone, no matter how many persons might be present. So if aloneness defines me, to go into the desert is to acknowledge that solitude is the most honest act that I can make. I have no right to hope for anything more than the courage to endure. There is something heroic about hermits daring to push human experience to the frontiers, striving to go beyond. I, too, yearn to find out what, if anything, transcends ordinary existence. Perhaps it is a good sign that I have come to recognize modern society as a conspiracy of busyness and noise to keep me from encountering my solitude. My failure here in the hermitage is driving me to the edge. At least for a while, I must have nothing and be nothing. Either that, or I will be driven into a more frantic drivenness to cover more nakedness than I thought I had, and to soothe my nausea over twisted motives in which everything has its seductive price.*

But the entrance fee for the desert comes perilously close to what I have struggled most of my life to avoid: depression, chaos, loneliness, foolishness, weakness, insecurity, limitedness, helplessness, contingency, the terror of nothingness—all these are variations on the themes of void and death. Here, in writing, I must confess my primary fear in being a hermit: that I will be nobody, with nobody knowing or caring. That's it. Straight!

I have read a host of books on the hermit life these past three months. I have talked with those who claim that on the other side of the desert, with arms stripped and hands empty, one receives back each moment of existence and every speck of the earth as gift. I read also that it happens in a manner that is least expected, with moments experienced for their own sake, beyond question and thus beyond answer. My head acknowledges this, but I do not know any of it. And so, for now, I will return to the monastery, holding onto this one hope: that in the desert, I will neither run nor be easily satisfied. Clearly, I would not have chosen this if I had had any choice."

Intermission
The Time Between:
Itself the Desert

I remember well my angry feelings at the end of my first stay at the hermitage. I clearly was not ready to be a hermit, no matter how much I wanted to be. And a huge intrusion postponed for three weeks my return to the monastery to begin preparations for trying again. The reason was that two years before, I had been offered an amazing opportunity: an all-expense-paid trip to Africa, with an opportunity for European travel. What at the time seemed to be a rare opportunity now intensified my failure, postponing any opportunity to redeem myself.

My longest time would be in Kenya at a world conference, followed by visits of my own choosing to Cairo, Jerusalem, Athens, Rome, Florence, Salzburg, and London.

I had a particularly hard night in my hermitage, the last night before my flight. This is the way my journal remembers it.

"I do not want to put me on hold any longer. I sense that I am beginning to know what I need to be about, but here I am, packing for the wrong place at the wrong time. The least I can do is to own up to what I am feeling. So I write this confession:

'*As a hermit, I have failed. I could defend myself by claiming insights gained, but it is to no avail. I dare not hide any longer from myself. I have lacked the will, the resolution, to persevere. If I am to make it, I must have a structure that is internalized, and a community with whom I can covenant to be held accountable.*'"

Before I left, I was reading Carl Jung. I summarized a section in my own words, to carry in my pocket during the trip, keeping alive the issue to which I must return.

Authentic life begins with the courage to withdraw all projections, thereby becoming conscious of one's own thick shadow. From then on, "they" will not be the primary enemy, for it is I who will become the serious problem for me. What is wrong in the world is what is wrong within my own bruised soul. Thus to deal with it is to care for one small part of today's unsolved social problems.

How profoundly this trip proved Jung to be right. Journaling has been an important vehicle of illumination thus far, and so it is for this trip. Rather than this adventure being a major distraction, it becomes a crucial part of my desert pilgrimage. In an important sense, the centerpiece of my adventure is an exhibit case at the museum in Nairobi, Kenya. Here in front of me is the earliest known human skull, "Lucy" by name. Although her fragments are unpretentiously cemented together, she still taunts me, insisting that human consciousness emerged at least two and a half million years ago. I am almost paralyzed by the questions posed by this skull. I look away, only to have my eyes caught by a surrounding mural depicting life as Lucy probably lived it. The impact is harsh. Our technological advances since then are obvious. Yet as I look, almost transfixed, one question becomes unavoidable. In terms of our spiritual evolution, have we taken even one step?

The stories I read this morning from the daily newspaper tucked under my arm are only a more sophisticated version of the exhibit. There they are, rudely staring back at me. They are my ancestors—throwing stones at territorial enemies, coveting possessions, and exploiting the weak. As much as I may want to, I cannot help concluding that these are common themes of being "human," binding our culture to theirs. It is hard to deny that Lucy and I both look out at the same sky, both of us with cosmic loneliness and ego needs as the drives that culminate time after time in either conquest or submission. In that sense, nothing really has changed, except the increasing destructiveness of the means.

Medieval monks were given a skull, sometimes their former cell-neighbor, on which to ponder the meaning of life. Lucy is that skull for me. She is my sister, separated not just by a piece of glass but a length of time beyond imagining. She is both unimposing and sphinxlike. We stared at each other, as if a gaze might ignite a recognition of comradeship. But what finally makes her inaccessible is my total inability to grasp the devastating agony of living and dying over the 2.5 million intervening years of human pilgrimage. Sticks and bombs, disease and healing, losers and winners, sadism and poetry, Madonna and Sodom. It is all here, in the silence, with Lucy's empty skull gawking at me. In another sense, it is suffering that welds us together. But for what? That is the question. If Lucy and I are sister and brother, all of history is undone—for who we were and who we are and who we yet will be are all basically the same, all of us caught in a maelstrom of unthinkable diameter, composed of more and more of the same.

I have no idea how long I am standing here. I feel trapped. Do I dare believe that the only meaning there might be is froth from innumerable intertwining circles, each and all bringing us back to where we started? If the promise that is the Kingdom of God means only that God will return us to Eden, I must hand back my entrance ticket. Millions of years, squandered for nothing, the agony, the suffering, in a purposeless cauldron of death. No! Can it be?

I want to break the glass, touch the skull, and embrace it as bone of my bones. Surely Lucy and I are both born to ask the same question of the same silent skies, as we find distraction by seeking a feeble security in quibbling over the same competitive diversions, astride the grave.

I walk out the front door. The museum door creaks as it closes behind me. I stumble out into the glaring sunlight, hoping to shake the encounter. Yet wherever I go, Lucy and I keep stumbling over each other—sometimes as grins, oftentimes staring at each other in disbelief. Our dance begins immediately, as soon as I am finally able to focus my eyes. Spread out in front of me is Nairobi's white exploitation, begun with the land's "discovery" in 1498 by Vasco de Gama, of grade school fame. Whites banished the natives from this cool plateau, pushing them into the steamy, deadly jungles. Black by biology, white by culture, Kenya depends on a tourism that puts wild animals in preserves to protect them from whites, so that underpaid blacks can drive whites in air-conditioned vans to resort balconies, where the whites can watch with moonlight cocktails as the animals attack each other at lighted salt-licks.

I am eating breakfast on the colonial terrace where Teddy Roosevelt once dined, while over five hundred black porters carried his supplies so that he could kill 296 wild animals. It is not a long walk from there to a vast cardboard city I find by chance, carefully placed out of the sight of tourists. It is where natives build their shacks near their food supply: the city dump.

On the hill overlooking it all is what appears to be a fortress. After a long climb, it identifies itself safely as an Anglican Church. Inside, the paradoxes again grin down on me. White-faced, stained-glass saints serenely give "eternal tribute" to the "young martyrs" of the English armed forces, who "contributed so selflessly in the South African Campaign," to the "black watch" and the "wars of defense." Meanwhile, somewhere in the affluent sector, at a place where the poor had been swept from the streets so as to impress the tourists, the speakers at my conference drone on, apparently oblivious to what is going on all around. Exquisite woodcarvings made by natives are sold at high prices in white shops for the tourists. I know I should not do it, but in one such place I ask if I can buy Lucy. The clerk does not understand.

The following day, on the outskirts of Cairo, Egypt, amidst a gauntlet of peddlers and hustlers and guides, I purchase for a "dollah" an entrance up a narrow shaft to the precise center of the Great Pyramid. Here in the sacred death chamber the intense silence can touch Eternity. And yet, the sacredness is naked, stripped bare, ravished not only of its furnishings but even the murals that once adorned its walls—stolen by the English to adorn their own museums. And the king, once revered as eternal, is no longer a resident here, where time bartered with immortality. He is in a glass cage in a museum where for an entrance fee tourists can exercise their curiosity by staring at his nakedness. Lest I appear a purist, I too paid the price, for nothing much seems to have changed.

Later, there is Jerusalem, or almost so, for I am delayed by Israeli guards who look askance at me for coming from a country with which they are not on speaking terms. With the afternoon sun hot against ancient walls, I am pressed by a throng through the Damascus Gate, into a strange world that appears not to have changed since Jesus haunted these streets. Having no idea of what to do or where to go, I spy a sign pointing toward a "Christian Tourist Office." In the lobby is a poster indicating a pilgrimage led by Franciscans along the Via Dolorosa every Friday at 3:00 PM. Today is Friday. It is now 3:00 PM. After quick directions, I race through cobble-stoned passageways, down ancient steps, toward the chanting. The pilgrimage now includes me, as we slowly pass merchants who are blatantly hostile to this religious intrusion upon their buying and selling. This is the path of which I have heard since a boy. Here it is, the cobble-stoned Way of the Cross, witnessing quietly to the painful passage of Jesus from condemnation to death. I am not a person of pious feelings, yet at some of the fourteen stops, I experience strange shivers of identity. Three times I pause to become recollected. Three times he falls.

The fourteen stations finally move us into an ancient church, up a steep pair of rock steps to the right. Everyone kneels. So do I. Then, one by one, each person moves forward to touch a hole in the rock floor under the altar. "What is that?" I whisper to the person next to me. "Where the cross was erected." "This is Golgotha?" "Shhh. Yes!" The real one? The place of the *skull*! I am not prepared. But before I am able to let that feeling mingle with all the other ones I am collecting, we go down another pair of stairs, into the nave. There we wait. For what? We stand in a single file, in front of a small structure that looks like a poorly constructed imitation cave. My turn comes. I bend down, entering into a tiny room. "What is this?" I whisper to the Franciscan monk sitting there. I tremble with his reply: "The sepulcher." *The* sepulcher? It is very silent. Like whitewashed death. When I reemerge, stumbling a bit, I move toward some darkness. Any darkness. A monk sees me and presses a rosary into my hand. "I think you need this. Persevere."

I find the exit door, and spend the evening sitting alone in Gethsemane, across the Kidron Valley from the city of God. I watch Jerusalem glowing in the sunset, its closest gate bricked up until the Messiah returns—or comes. Night sounds compete, noisily: Muslim, Jewish, Christian—Orthodox, Armenian, Roman Catholic. Then it becomes very quiet, except for an occasional gunshot. Beneath an ancient olive tree, thought by some to be *the* spot, a small plaque encounters me. These are its words: "I do not understand you, but I trust you." I am home.

The Acropolis in Athens is best visited by sunrise. Here, in contrast to yesterday's teeming throngs trying to buy and sell Zion, is the unparalleled monument to reason's hope for ordering the passions. At its heart is the rational simplicity of the crumbling Parthenon, its adornments likewise stolen to become the main showpiece of the British Museum. What remains are only the architectural bones of temples to gods and goddesses remembered only in worn guidebooks. And quietly below rests the over-turned stones where Socrates once walked the marketplace, condemned as subversive for insisting on asking "Why?"

From there the pilgrimage leads to Rome. Here the same basic paradox prevails. This time it centers on a people who think that they are building for eternity, sifting the Semitic heart through the Grecian mind as foundation for an empire. Standing in the center of the hulking space called St. Peter's, I turn in all directions, very slowly, trying to take it in. Tertullian's question becomes my whisper: "What has Jerusalem to do with Athens . . . or Egypt . . . or this?"

Questions are beginning to weigh like crosses hung around my neck. What am I to do with the glorious results that occur when the "Vicar of Christ" insists that Raphael must paint the walls and ceilings of his own private sleeping quarters? I reach the paradoxical jewel— the Sistine Chapel. My eyes are drawn immediately to the ceiling's center point, where the finger of God and of Adam almost touch. From that moment, creation tumbles forth with history's tempestuous strivings finally plunging downward onto the far wall. There the figures once full and vibrant with promise become contorted and twisted by the viciousness of self-interest. This is Michelangelo's final tragic judgment on the whole human pilgrimage. I walk Rome's streets that afternoon, passing monument after monument in honor of a city's plunder and subjugation.

Then there is Florence, the fresh promise of a new world optimistically called the Renaissance. Here a synthesis of Christianity and humanism ignites the likes of Dante, Michelangelo, Giotto, Botticelli—and Machiavelli. Yet the competitive individualism of this amazing collection of artistic genius, gathered by the Medici family, becomes a cloak hiding political viciousness. And here it happens again. Christianity births a Savonarola, who with silver tongue and ascetic presence masterfully condemns the corruption of both church and state—until power moves into his own grasp. Becoming a dictator in his own right, he is not only hanged, but burned at the stake. Wherever I go, it is as though my paradoxical walk through history repetitively discloses an ongoing desert plot. And at night Lucy's skull is rarely absent.

Today is Salzburg. Arriving in time for the Mozart Festival, I expect things to be more promising. But again the persistent paradox reechoes. This time it begins at Mozart's birthplace. Let me confess some arrogance by insisting that very little of human creativity is beyond my capacity to conceive. Mozart is the exception. Spoiled, egotistic, with more than a touch of perversion, from him emerges a beauty that can only have emerged in spite of him, as sheer gift. How else can I understand a person who at age three plays the clavier, creates a symphony at age six, composes in most musical forms by age eight, and in his prime could compose multiple symphonies at the same time in his head? The paradox this time becomes visual. Here in the glass case before me is the violin upon which this tiny child once thrilled royalty. And beside it is his bow, a "misfit" for his instrument.

Wherever I go, each place folds in upon itself to form the same paradoxical circle. At each of history's intersections there is a Jericho road between Sodom and the Madonna, along which walks a passionate child with a misfit bow.

Finally I reach England, that outreach of Christian expansion which birthed my own ancestors. Here royalty, ambition, church, greed, empire, slavery, poetry, bishops, colonialism, adventure, crown jewels, and strategic beheadings coalesce into what I have been taught to call "civilization." I walk slowly the Thames at sunset, listening as Big Ben chimes, as if tolling a requiem for an empire that has touched with arrogance every place I had visited.

What enigmatic victories they are—conquering in the name of the cross, evangelizing on behalf of profit, with stolen land defended by forts named after the saints. It all fits, yet nothing does. On this evening along the Thames I feel something happening to me. I feel the draining marks of aging, of me and of history, in a final and fatal loss of innocence. Powerfully I recall the day before this adventure began. I stood as a soiled failure in the middle of a simple hermitage. This night in London I discover that I did not stand there alone.

My crescendo is Stonehenge. Here ancient ponderings about sacred mysteries are acted out to the rhythms of the eternal spheres, around a timeless center. Lucy's skull in Kenya to these boulders of Stonehenge in England seems like a far distance. But soon after I pay the entrance fee, I discover it turns out to be no step at all. No one is permitted to go anywhere near the stones, which are well guarded by a fence. "Why?" I ask. The guard is precise. "We can't trust anyone up close any more. They carve vulgar stuff all over the rocks." This is the benediction to my journey.

I hope that the drive from my little Missouri airport to my tiny monastery in the Ozarks will provide the distance I need. All through the flight home I feel overwhelmed. Instead, it is twilight as I pass through hills once lush with forests. Now they are poverty strickened, stripped naked by the lumber barons a century ago, left to erode into marginality, barely supporting the poor that hang on. At the monastery door, I pause, trying to bring some closure before joining my brothers in sleep. What do I know now? I know now how deeply each of us is a microcosm of history. My three-week pilgrimage through history has not distracted me from the sense of personal failure with which I left. What happened is that wherever I went, I was confronted by my own face-to-face enigma writ large. Certainly I will remain involved in social justice. But from now on I shall do so with the sad knowing that on the human plane *every change and every advance simply poses more graphically the paradox of human existence.* My trip did not postpone my reentry into the desert. Rather, it disclosed history as being itself the desert.

3

✿ Preparing to Reenter the Desert

I returned to the monastery, chastened and perhaps sadly wiser. I have carefully selected excerpts from my nine-month journal that describe well my formation during the weeks of my second try at monastic preparation. The dates are from the original journal entries. This, then, is my second crash course. I call it Hermitage 102.

Saturday, August 16, 1986

It is only halfway through August, and already the dawns are becoming crisp. The birds will be migrating soon. I am determined to learn in these final weeks of formation what I need in order to enter into my own winter solitude. This morning it seems that an appropriate place for re-beginning is to read Merton's Day of a Stranger. *In this book he describes a typical day in his hermitage.*

It is evening now. I finished his description. Merton conveys a deep sense of happiness, of coming home. Finally he is able to cash in his excessive obligations for a goodly supply of immediacy. He and his life are both at their best when he does pure description. Almost poetic are his words about simple routines as liturgy, daily objects as friends, and the creatures of nature as his "choir companions."

The beauty of his writings emerges when he can permit them to breathe the gentle hints of one deeply bruised. Not surprisingly, the relationship of both of us to God echoes the same plot—one of absence and aloneness, with only a hint of presence. The causative figure in my life has thus far refused to make a visible guest appearance. But I am beginning to sense through Merton what is ahead for me.

"So, Paul," I ask myself, "what would an ideal day at the hermitage look like for you?" I can imagine awaking while it is still night, and walking outside through the sounds of silence, unafraid, at peace. Inside, there might be a candle by an icon, the darkness woven with the lonely cries of coyotes. In fact, let me borrow Merton's phrase: "To hear one central tonic note to which pine, wind and bird ascend or descend in melody." But I am not ready. The ideal would be if some day the sacred hours could be enfolded by a chorus of gentle memories purged of the ominous cries from a past that I have sealed off selectively with caution. There, I said it. Healing must involve "returning to the woods where I am nobody."

Monday, August 18

Most of my readings thus far have been from Roman Catholic sources. Today I attempt to discover the Protestant counterpart. This afternoon I have a better sense of the Reformation perspective. Intriguingly, it is built upon the etymology of the word prayer, meaning asking or begging.

Thus for Luther, the heart of prayer is dialogue, intent, if need be, on changing God's mind. What a contrast to the liberalism I have known, in which only the person praying can be changed. This dilutes the value of prayer totally to the subjective, for the intention is to help the person accept the unchangeable by changing one's own attitude. With the Reformers, however, prayer affects outcomes that would not otherwise occur, for God responds when asked. This makes prayer a courageous effort of will, more exhausting than all other types of work.

God meets us, Emil Brunner says, at the limits of our knowledge and our power, waiting in the desert *where it is fearful to be alone with God. Wherever I turn, Catholic or Protestant, I keep encountering the word* desert. *Certainly at Gethsemane, Jesus' desert prayer is a pleading for his life, intent on changing God's mind. And when after three separate times this does not occur, he charges God with abandonment: "My God, why. . . ." The Vigil psalms this morning express such praying: "My God I call for help by day . . . and I cry at night before you." Other such expressions jump out at me. "I have reached the end of my strength." "I am drowned beneath your waves." "You have taken away my friends." "Why do you hide your face?" "Your terrors have utterly destroyed me." And finally, "My one companion is darkness."[1]*

I stay in the monastery chapel a long time tonight, with a solitary light focused upon the crucifix. The prayer life I need requires a God with whom I can contend, because that God is contending with that which destroys our humanity. Far more than asking, I need a God with whom I can complain and question and confront. If this is what prayer is, long have I wanted it! My God, why death, catastrophes, suffering, and abandonment? Such praying could stalk the perimeters, from pleading to angry contesting, in a dogged effort to outlast God's will.

Back in my cell, as the Great Silence brings finality to the day, I begin to realize why prayer might be so difficult for me. It means asking, but, as a depression child, I was never allowed to ask for anything. With little to go around, I had to trust that my parents were doing the best they could. Only once did I speak out about what I wanted. I was a child at the "five-and-dime" store. I spied a little wooden engine with two cars. My little heart drowned in covetousness. I ached for it. I cried for it. After several heavy swats to the backside, I was carried bodily from the store. There, humiliated at curbside, I vowed never to want anything again. In the growing dark, I realize now that I have never asked for anything since. And if I cannot ask, then I am out of touch with what I want. Somehow all this seems to have much to do with my search for God, even though I am one of those men who does not ask for directions.

As the moon begins its ascent, I sense that a life of prayer is not a posture of weakness or whining, as often portrayed, but one of considerable bravery. Jacob could be my model, daring to wrestle God to a draw. Instead of God being his crutch, God caused his limp. So, I fear, might be the case with me. Jacob never again walked without the marks of the desert—and thus of his God.

Tuesday, August 19

I awake to the 3:15 AM bells with a clear image. It is as though my mind has been working all night. Prayer is "holy desperation." Contention is not an act of prideful disbelief, which had been my suspicion. It is at the heart of prayer. No wonder I have had problems with spirituality. My image of prayer life has been one of weakness—of being effeminate, feeble, impoverished, and needy. What a contrast it is to understand the one who prays as being importunate, defiant, intent on wearing God out with insistence and long-suffering. Jesus himself praised the persistent widow as a model for our prayerful relationship with God. I remember Teresa of Avila's indictment: "I do not wonder, God, that you have so few friends from the way you treat them."

Later, as I sit on the back kitchen steps watching the morning make its move, I recall the character named Cleo in Anderson Herrell's Where She Was. *In meeting the God of a Protestant Church, she laughs: "He's too nice." In contrast, the only God she knows either "breaks down your door or passes your house by." The God with whom the Reformers contend is the one who specializes in door kicking. Yet, I must confess, at this point in my pilgrimage, I would find animated protest silly, maybe psychotic. It would be like yelling at a closed door, demanding that it open. The God with whom I seem to specialize is either the one who does not exist, or the one who has long since passed by my house. It is difficult sometimes to know the difference.*

I screw down the lid on my thinking, and ride a bicycle as hard as I can, as far as I can, until I reach the cliffs overlooking

Bryant Creek. I laugh until it echoes. Then I sit down and taste the morning.

Wednesday, August 20

Today brings its own dose of uneasiness. Yesterday's image of prayer as a vigorous kind of desert dialogue is gnawing at the last feeble images of the God that I thought I had. There seems to be a fatal shallowness to the God of my liberal theological heroes, whether Paul Tillich, J. A. T. Robinson, or Matthew Fox. Since their God cannot act, or be changed, or influenced, prayer is restricted to human ascent, not Divine descent.

All day I muse over the need for an alternative image of God, different from both my childhood image and those from my graduate days. I want no longer to bootleg both into the present. How am I to understand why Luther prayed three to four hours a day, and Calvin insisted upon raising the same supplication to God a thousand times, if necessary. My feeble efforts at prayer are damningly general, while those of the Reformers are etched with proper names, cured in the sweat of identifiable settings. No wonder they gambled their lives on prayer's consequences. Spirituality and the desert for them seem to be nearly identical.

By Compline time, paradox reemerges as the only way to express the Divine-human relationship. It is a matter of violent gentleness, battering at doors that may be unlocked, cursing with loving intercessions. The person of prayer is a living pietà.

Friday, August 22

It is becoming cold. Good soup weather. Appropriately my monastic assignment today is to be cook. There is something therapeutic about taking leftovers and vegetables of questionable longevity, and rendering a fine soup out of such marginality. I chuckle that such transubstantiation may link stove and altar. What a shame if God cannot taste soup. Or watch the fog gathering in the valley at daybreak. Or embrace a brother at Eucharist. What a tragic difference if God only knows about such things. Surely Incarnation means that God tastes from within. And given the withered ingredients we provide, God must be an extraordinary soup maker! But if by chance God cannot taste his own brew, I shall taste it for him—or her.

Since returning to the monastery, I have been doing faithfully all the things that a monk does—seven daily offices, two periods of work, and daily Eucharist. The rest of the time I have been reading, voraciously. My reading today feels desperate, scrambling for a viable image of the God I am seeking. I explore some of the saints for clues. I am strangely drawn to Saint Theresa of Lisieux, even though I expected the worst. She is traditionally pictured with pink angel cherubs gathered around her bed, as she experiences an early death with joyous serenity. I choose her, grudgingly, for no other reason than that she is a favorite saint of the monks here, and, in fact, Merton dedicated his life to her. My hope is that her childlikeness might peel from me the sophistication that has atrophied whatever it might mean to experience God.

I am surprised. Wafting through Theresa's life is my own haunting theme—the silence of God. Nearing her death from tuberculosis, she describes her soul as "enveloped in a thick darkness." Replacing her previous intimacies with God is an "unbroken silence." The accompanying feelings of being "unloved and rejected" are not simply a temporary reversal caused by intense suffering. Throughout her final year, she continues to be haunted by a "fear of doubt." This is so central, she says, that it makes of everything "a land of fog" where "one feels lost." "It has all faded away!" she cries. How can one "look forward to death," she laments, when "it will give you not what you hope for, but a night darker still, the night of utter nothingness? To write more might be blasphemy."

Toward the end of her life, she confesses experiencing "a wall that reaches to the very heavens, shutting out the starry sky." In reading this next sentence, something happens to me: "When I sing in my poems of the happiness of heaven and of the eternal possession of God, I feel no joy. I sing only of what I wish to believe." *This is why* "I have made more acts of faith *during the past year than in all the rest of my life." Theresa is my sister, for she too is the disciple of the "nevertheless." Close to death, she put such matters clearly: "How I have been tempted during this night. But I never ceased making acts of faith." The approach of death reduces faith to its essential: an act of courage in the face of all evidence to the contrary. She knows this well: "When I cry to heaven for help, it is then that I feel most abandoned." Abandoned. Yes, she knows.*

I had begun reading Theresa with skepticism over what I thought I would find in the romanticized and sanitized "saintly" Theresa, dying in "transports of love." Instead, I ended with the real Theresa, who is, in fact, a saint. Grasping her crucifix, she dies this way: "Now, in the face of death, gathering all her strength, all her faith, all her love, she voiced with her last breath her vehement protest that the silence of God had not touched her faith nor diminished her love...." Then she releases her hold on life, uttering the ultimate paradox as a "will to believe," as her own life's translation of Jesus' final words: "My God, I love you."[2] I find a picture of her taken shortly after death. I have fallen in love.

Saturday, August 23

Today is important. Theresa remains near. Spirituality for her depends not upon experience at all but on praxis, not on emotion but will. I have felt "unspiritual" most of my own life because I could not really say that I have experienced God. Yet right now I am not even sure what that would mean. Nonetheless, even if I had an undeniable experience of God, one would not be able to make it normative for all believers. Such experiences are rare, evidently available only to the few, if at all. So the real question is what sustains even these few when they are in the desert, straddled between such rarities? I am discovering that faith is the same for them as it is for the rest of us. The heart of faith is a willed obedience, with discipline being the only way to survive faithfully through the lifelong desert.

The Daily Offices are the Church's gift to God, called the opus Dei, the work of us for God. This discipline is what forms the self, not so much as what to think, but as how to do so.

*These seven prayer liturgies each day are meant for all
Christians, as the discipline that makes theologizing a way of
life. They must become the backbone of my hermit experience,
as a map for the desert. Knowing means acting as if, with repetition being the rehearsal by which we can begin to see, hear,
touch, smell, and taste in a uniquely Christian way. The second
nature that results makes it possible to experience everything as
gift. I am getting close.*

*By Compline time, things seem simple, and thus terribly
hard. I have known gracious, priceless moments in the past. I
have also known times of frightening abandonment. Can it be
that faith, after all, is not a matter of experiencing something
new?* Is it not a matter of *wagering on* what kind of experience
one will live as primal, *with the contrary kind becoming one's
conundrum? Either way is a gamble. Each has its evidence. But
each also has missing pieces. Thus I must make a primal choice,
with all else being the practiced determination to see through the
glasses of that choice.* Yes, but *strangely at this moment I do not
feel that I have a choice. The choice has chosen me—to become
a hermit in the desert that I do not desire to enter.*

Sunday, August 24

*What is drawing me outside each morning is the playful
mist collecting in the valley below. Today is the Sabbath. So I do
more than watch the fog. I walk into it, and over it, and with it.
The sun keeps poking its finger through it, desirous of shaking
hands with anything touchable. I stay too long. When I return
at sunset, there is a note on my door: "Warm pizza waiting for*

you in the oven." Then a whisper at the beginning of Vespers: "We missed you." To be wanted, to be accepted, to belong. That feeds me so deeply, as the opposite of abandonment. Grace is the name for such acceptance. I wonder what the name and face are for the abandonment.

Monday, August 25

After lunch, I stretch out on the grass, as wind and sun play counterpoint against my skin. It is clear that until I can claim a viable image of God on the basis of which to gamble, prayer will remain vague, and even a nuisance. And without prayer as powerfully viable, God is a less honest word than Nothingness. I feel relief in finally being able to state the issue—or one of them.

Vespers is softly appealing, especially the humble honesty of the spontaneous prayers of intercession. In contrast to this morning's Scripture in which the angry God kills everyone in sight, I keep staring at the crucifix. Its loincloth wraps us all together—Golgotha and concentration camps, starving children and abandoned lovers. Rooted together in such pain and anger, the intercessions this evening glow with deep inevitability. Tonight, for a timeless moment, a tiny group of white-robed monks, unknown to the world, whisper together in the gathering twilight, becoming contemporaneous with all suffering, past and present. I walk out into the evening, knowing why Christian prayer always ends "in the name of Christ." Life as a procession marching to the death chamber is madness—unless it is the crucified one who is leading the way.

Tuesday, August 26

*A few days ago, someone left May Sarton's Journal of a
Solitude on the library table. I opened it randomly. The first
sentence I read snared me: "I hope to break through into the
rough, rocky depths, to the matrix itself. There is violence there
and anger never resolved. My need to be alone is balanced
against my fear of what will happen when suddenly I enter the
huge empty silence and I cannot find support there."³ After
frightening me, she begins to meddle. "I hardly ever sit still without being haunted by the 'undone' and the 'unsent.' I often feel
exhausted." She is my desert friend.*

*I am hooked. All day long I discover that she knows
personally all my favorite distractions for shielding me from me.
But she, too, knows as well the silent peace of sacramental
moments—the perfume of damp soil, a drink of sherry over
memories, a chance note by a stranger, a cup of raspberries as a
surprise gift to a friend, the hopeful liturgy of autumn bulb-
planting, the hills as old friends, a special meal for an even more
special companion, smoke and falling leaves, the melancholy of
light in the fall, beeches of transparent gold, and each first
snow. These are the moments when life asks for me, too, by my
first name. She is my sister.*

*That is why she is not able to fool me in those sections
when she postures an appearance of outward calm. She gives
hints all along that moments of happiness and touches of love
only intensify her longing without and her thirsting within. As
poets, we both stand on the dizzy edge of things. We are the
burned ones, damned and yet blessed by the burden of Mystery*

as a "*Divine discontent.*" So smitten, she recognizes the landmarks of the territory that I, too, know by heart—tormented self-depression, raging anger, fear of silence. And so her heights are spiced by crying, her longings with exhaustion, and her depths with self-doubts.

As I continue to read during the noontime siesta, perched on my favorite log in the woods, two conflicting images about Sarton wrestle my mind to a draw. One is the streak of wildness with which she cherishes a piece of land, fighting it into a semblance of order and beauty. The other is the cut flowers she purchases and brings into her hermitage so as never to forget how ephemeral is all such effort. If the two of us could unpack that paradox, the sphinx would be robbed of its riddle.

By evening, May has broken out of her month-long depression with an important realization: "That a middle-aged single woman, without any vestige of family left, lives in this house in a silent village and is responsible only to her own soul means something."

Wednesday, August 27

Today is a terrible day. I am not sure what to make of it. It seems that whenever things begin to make sense, I awaken with biting doubts. "God satisfies the empty soul," said the psalmist at Vigils. Really? And at Lauds God promises: "Open wide your mouth and I will fill it." Not so.

This morning I rearrange my desk yet another time, into piles of things to be done. Honesty would have labeled them as

"Things I Do Not Want to Do." Today everything feels heavy with obligation.

Yet in a quiet moment, the monastic cook shares that he had wanted to grow a garden outside the kitchen, but was never given permission. "I'll have a garden at my hermitage for both of us," I reply. I am surprised by how quickly those words come. I have not gardened since I was a child. I kept pestering my father until he gave me a tiny patch of my own to plant, to keep me from tramping on his. I remember still the smell of summer greenness when I would sit on the squishy earth between two tomato plants, trying to feel them grow. Yes, the hermitage will have growing things.

One of the psalms at Vespers begins with the words "I will seek the Lord; I will seek [God] all my life." Seek, oh yes. I am trying. I am an obedient monk, I really am. I do everything I am told. But is this seeking? Each morning at Eucharist I watch the monks come. I watch the monks go. I see kindness. I hear gentleness. They respond to a common bell, and their responsibilities are shared by all for all. Other than that, each is really on his own. Outwardly there is a quiet simplicity, order, and dignity. But behind each set of eyes, back where human ambiguity sets up shop, I know very little. These are my friends, but I do not know who any of them are. Or even what each of them does, really. I have a dangerous urge to unscrew the head of my nearest local monk, peer inside, and gently demand, "What are you doing down in there!" I suspect that there is a desert down there, too.

The days are shortening. Compline in summer is alive with twilight color. But for the last several evenings, there has been barely enough light to see the psalms. Soon this office will be by memory in the darkness. Whatever happens, the seasons keep changing, with or without me.

Tonight during benediction it strikes me that I need an overnight dress rehearsal, as it were, in one of the monastic hermitages, armed with little more than paper and a pencil. And a seeking soul.

Thursday, August 28

I am beginning to recognize graced moments. Sky, eyes, streams, birds. To say "yes" to living seems so simple, yet I still have to work at it. My hermit spiritual director lives each day as if it were a Sabbath. Appropriately, he invited me to his hermitage this Sunday. I am to bring the wine. There is something there that he knows and I need to know. Almost like a mantra, when I see him I keep repeating, "He knows."

This afternoon I yearn for music. Yet in looking through the records in the music room, I cannot do it. For the first time, it seems contrived to choose a particular piece and label this fragment of my life "music time." I no longer know quite what to do with sequential time. Instead, I fantasize hearing a Bach Brandenburg Concerto on a tape deck while bouncing along an Ozark road in a red pickup at sunrise, going nowhere in particular.

Today is bread day. A special intimacy develops between the dough and me. It is an event of rising, aroma, and color. Sitting at sunrise on the kitchen steps, I proclaim hot coffee and fresh bread to be the primal sacrament. The only rival is the priestly act of making soup. The celery crunch, the sym-

metry of onion rings, the arrogant redness of tomatoes—a mystic could get lost in such things.

My bedtime reading contributes for my sleep the image of liturgy as play, inviting each person to an eternal childhood with God. Because worship has no purpose, it is full of Divine meaning. The last sentence I remember reading came as another desert call: "The soul must learn to abandon . . . the restlessness of purposeful activity; it must learn to waste time for the sake of God." That will be the mark of my healing.

Friday, August 29

In three weeks I will be in my hermitage. Last week I promised my spiritual director that I would keep asking myself, "What do I really want?" Now I know. I really do. I want to be whole, to be released from the cocoon of self-canceling longings. I want seeds planted in paper cups to adorn my windowsills. And music—to play it, to write it, and to try dancing it. And I want to be drawn outside. "Outside" in the past has always functioned as a reward for dutifully doing inside what I did not want to do. I still hear the voice, "But is your room clean?" By the time my "doing" buys me some guiltless moments, I am too tired to enjoy them. Yes, I want to be free to go outside—outside as the inside of everything.

I just found an apt name for my life thus far: postponed living. My time is largely instrumental—yesterday is for today because today is for tomorrow. What a contrast this is with hermit time, where life is lived one day at a time, each moment equidistant from nowhere and everywhere, its breadth measured *by its depth. Aging seems to be a peeling away of the sequential kind of time, onionskin by onionskin. But what I suspect is that my peeling will finally come to the empty center where a fortune cookie reads, "Too late!"*

My colleagues will ask me, "What did you accomplish on your sabbatical?" Do I dare reply, "The monks made me wave at the birds—to the glory of God"?

Saturday, August 30

At daybreak, I begin writing the epiphanies that have emerged through my dialoguing with Sarton, wisdom that I can take with me to my hermitage. She and I are walking paradoxes: clutching lyric moments as a way of warding off the panic of failure; giving to others as a battering for attention, while being suffocated by the burden when others respond; thumbing our noses at death, while being more than a little in love with it; caught between intensity and distance, doing and being, prophet and hermit. And so, to be changed, I must go unprotected. My companion will be the Divine Presence experienced as absence. Joy will have about it a touch of flirtation with death. Savoring each thing will relate to the ability to let it go. One particular image of hers will remain: that of cut flowers by fireside in defiance of the blizzard raging noisily outside. I must write to her.

As I go to Terce, a whippoorwill sings. It is late in the season for a mating call. Its lonely call wraps itself around the crucifix on the front wall. Both are calls for a lost companion.

This afternoon I meet with the Abbot. He, too, knows what I need to know. His opening words are stern. "If you do not practice holy leisure here, why come? We need to force you to waste time. Merton was like you—always reading, with a second book in his pocket. But he was terribly disciplined. He set aside times to do nothing." I ask the Abbot how he does that himself. "My morning time between Vigils and Lauds is holy. I would never think of working, writing, or reading then. This is the time for being present to Presence." He spends this time in his cell, often in the dark. "I'll even take a nap if that seems called for. Most people make love in bed. Why shouldn't that be a special place for celibates to experience spiritual intimacy?" One hour of such "disengagement" is his limit. "Then I pace." In his former hermitage, he completed the whole Psalter weekly as he walked back and forth. And after engagements with people, he became recentered through this same pacing, with rhythmic breathing. "That is the purpose of liturgy, psalms, Scripture, and the rosary. They are means for becoming wholly present again. I don't have to use such practices anymore, unless I get distracted."

I am curious about his call to be a monk and a hermit. It began as a youth when he was stopped by this thought: "If God is who the Church says God is, it is absurd not to be full time in God's presence. So I offered up everything for that Presence—my self, my talents, even work itself." "What would you tell me to do if I were your novice?" "Each monk must find his own way, but you need regular Sabbath days in which to do nothing. Echo these with shorter periods each day." His marching orders are perceptive. "Declare the Sabbath off-limits, making it for God alone, without compromise. Disarm yourself. I mean no book, no paper, no options but to be. Everything must be in the now." He anticipates my objection: "*You will be haunted by thinking that this is a waste of time. But imagine what you would be doing if you were not 'being.' You will be amazed at how insignificant it is in the larger picture.*"

He recalls Father Matthew Kelty's comment that "*the demon for the hermit is boredom.*" "*I've never been bored!*" I reply. "*Then that is where you have to begin. Go get bored to the glory of God!*" He makes my assignment clear: I am to waste time deliberately, as a forced feeding.

Sunday, August 31

I awake with clarity. My head is coming to understand monastic life. The reason why I resist doing nothing is that I am afraid of being nothing—so I run from my true self. I know as well that contemplation is the mark of the transformed desert life, as communion with a hidden God. Also I know that the demon to be overcome is the one who makes me feel guilt in relaxing and resting in darkness. And finally, what is the benefit of living the hermit life? It is to be able to live well with one's own self, for a lifetime.

But I only know these things with my head. I confess that after hearing the Abbot's instructions yesterday, what did I do? Just the opposite. Hardly realizing what I was doing, I went to the library and read about the Sabbath. I strongly suspect that the reason why I worked so hard reading and doing research yesterday was so that I would feel less guilt for doing nothing today! "Doing" is such an aggressive, greedy, and obsessive creature, refusing to wait its turn. Sunday is the day in which I have tried to have Sabbaths, but even so, I do it for the wrong reasons. Because most persons have Sunday off, I do not have to work so hard today in order for me to feel comparatively justified in taking some time off! This is hard to confess. Will this nonsense ever stop?

And yet my research has helped me gain a firmer sense of what Sabbath life might mean. The author who made this most graphic for me calls it sanctified leisure, *so running the length and breadth of living that it links creatively life's daily polarities: of being and doing, playing and working, desert and city, uselessness and usefulness, letting go and engagement, home and journey, passion and compassion, vertical and horizontal, feminine and masculine, Sabbath and ministry. I know now that without weekly Sabbath time, pastors like me are a nuisance to themselves and a menace to their congregations.*

So I try today to live a Sabbath, only to discover that my capacity for Sabbath lightness is directly proportional to the shortness of the time that I set aside as Sabbath. I even fumble over the right verb to say this. Set aside time to do what? To spend it? Relinquish it? Squander it? Yet I am beginning to sense what it would be like to live a moment, any moment, without duration. In fact, I think that if I could ever "take no thought for the morrow," I could be lured into the depth of a timeless now. I understand, but in understanding, I am recognizing as well the size of the blockage marked "baggage." It is rooted in part in my Puritan upbringing. As a child, Sunday was no Sabbath, for it was laced with restrictions. There were no Sunday newspapers, no purchasing, no cooking, no playing—just church, morning and evening. Only now am I becoming aware that such restrictions, as rooted in their biblical beginnings, are for a positive purpose: to free one from work in order to be freed for celebration, enjoying the Creator through tasting the creation.

It is an hour later. I got tired of my own internal babbling. So I went to the library for a book of pictures, convinced that it would have no possible utility. The one that chose me contained pictures of the Ozark Mountains, with short commentaries. The pictures begin wavering through my tears. I understand better now why I have come to this place in search of a home—because most of the folks living in these hills are displaced Appalachians, such as I. As I roam these hills through the picture book, I begin to reclaim my "geography of perspective." In the Rockies, one goes up and then down. In the Ozarks, one goes down and then up. We live and travel the ridges, looking out over the valleys. The theological implication of this insight floats in and out, but I do not bite. I stop reading the captions without even realizing it. I just sit, for a long time.

This afternoon I take the steep trail to the top of the hill, where my spiritual director's hermitage is perched at the edge of a pine forest. I knew it would be small, but not this small! The interior, barely large enough for the two of us, is dominated by a picture window over a desk. It looks down through a clearing, to knobs of wooded hills bouncing toward the horizon.

We make two toasts. The first is to solitude. The second is to friendship. We are a fine pair. My curiosity goes exploring. There is neither electricity nor running water, only a propane cooking burner and a wood-burning stove. His bed is abnormally high, designed for storing canned goods beneath. Several *storage compartments and an old stuffed chair complete the décor. The hermitage, which is no more than ten feet by twelve, has two foci. One is the window-desk. The second, built into the opposite wall over the bed, is a tabernacle with the reserved host. These two center his prayer life.*

The life of a hermit is becoming clearer. I can begin to imagine it. I had expected to feel cramped in his tiny hermitage. Instead, the tangible silence has the feel of intimacy and warmth, packaged in gentleness. In fact, what I am experiencing is close to what as a child I sensed in my tree house, and in the special moments for healing bruised feelings when I would hide under the front porch. It is like Elisha's room described in the Bible—built by a couple so that he could belong to the family. It is childlike, womb-shaped, and soul-size. Here a person could play "life," for one would not be tempted to take one's self too seriously.

We discuss kindly my failures. I begin to sense that what I really need is to experience a sacred space such as this. Even my confession illuminates the contours of my longing. His window especially draws me. I am sitting at the desk in front of the window as we talk, but I keep being drawn to look through it. It is like an opening out onto the whole earth. On a hill such as this, it would make sense to do as he does, interceding on behalf of all the world's needs and its sufferings.

We talk about his life. His hesitancy to share it is due neither to shyness nor false humility. It is just that his life is so simple, so repetitive, so much a part of who he is, that he does not feel that there is much of importance to talk about. In being drawn toward hermit existence, I have been haunted by the utilitarian question: "What good does it do?" But here in his quiet presence, the question becomes reversed. It is I and my frenetic pace who need to be the recipients of that question. At my insistence, we review his typical day. I know it by heart, but I want to picture it here where it happens. His 1:30 AM rising time sounds even more impossible than before. He has no communal support. The seven daily monastic offices form the skeleton of his life. Reading from Scripture plus some spiritual classics are his daily food.

His style of spirituality? I find that a four-word sentence suffices: "Being in the Presence." Even as a child, he knew that this was what he wanted. We are so different. He has a natural introverted temperament for a life which by nature seems inaccessible to me. Yet these differences are what draw us together. He seems to glow—his eyes, his walk. He is a bearded boy in love with his God. He can savor without holding on. Herein is our basic difference. He expressed it this way: "On life's pilgrimage, you want to savor everything along the path, while I am content just to be passing through." I sense another difference. I am learning how to love life as God's gift, while he has learned how to love God for the sake of the loving.

Up to this time, however, I have been given only hints about myself. So, inappropriately, I ask: "What does a person do whose life is simply 'to be'?" "I cut bread, sit, pray, look out the window, nod, do the offices, eat bread, and walk." I persist. "But what are you really doing when you do all those things?" "Nothing."

As I prepare to leave, I try to answer my own question about him. It would have something to do with that window. As

I keep looking, its mystery focuses on its invitation to "look out upon." Finally he tells me what I needed to know. "That is where I celebrate the Eucharist daily on behalf of the whole of creation." We finally part with an embrace. I had visited a holy place, where my friend has wisely chosen the better part—the joy of losing himself in God.

I walk home by sunset. The phrase "holy person" jiggles in my head, like change in my pocket. Back at the monastery, I look up the word "holy." It means neither "pure" nor "moral," as I had thought. Holy means "whole." That fits. I am learning. Wholeness is not achieved by doing. It is that out of which one's doing comes. That would mean that the only good is the "holy will," a purity of intention. And what is its test? I think I know—to do the good even if no one will ever know.

This has been a fine day, capped off after Compline by walking softly under a full moon. The shadows are translucent, within and without. The demons I fight will not roar. They just eat quietly, nibbling at the corners. But in the sacred silence of this monastery, they are beginning to take on shape—somehow having to do with "when," "after," and "just as soon as." Soon, very soon, they will have faces, too.

Wednesday, September 3

In several days we will celebrate Mary's birth. She has fourteen feasts in all, sprinkled throughout the church year. The most difficult of these for someone raised as a Protestant is her title as "the Mother of God." That phrase has always stopped me short, but today I find that it does so intriguingly.

I do not trust an all-male group. Without a feminine presence, vulgarity and competitive cockiness seem inevitable. Yet this all-male monastery is different, and I suspect that Mary is part of that difference. In robes resembling nightgowns, we men begin and end our days singing a love song to our bride, queen, and mother. And even this monastery itself is named for her: Assumption Abbey. Last night, as we chanted our last words of the day as a song to Mary, I found myself rocking back and forth, almost as if I were being rocked to sleep. Somehow it is as though the God I need is maternal. "A weaned child on its mother's breast, even so is my soul" (Ps. 131:2 Grail).

After Compline, as always, we file out of the chapel into death's "Great Silence." Monks are given only one day at a time, so this is the time to hand back our day, we hope with increase. We are given strength to face our nightly dying, for the Abbot sprinkles us with holy water, reminding us that in our baptism we have participated in Christ's death and resurrection. Our death is behind us. But on this particular night it is as though I am making a sleepy reentry into the primal womb. The illumination evoked in me is the feeling that resurrection might have something to do with being rocked in "the everlasting arms." Can it be, after all, that my crying out to the silent darkness is not so much for answers as it is a crying out to be held? I am getting close.

Thursday, September 4

After lunch, I go outside with meritorious resolve. My sole purpose is to feel the sun and clouds play hot-and-cold running tag on my face. Thoughts of wasted time drift by, but I nudge them aside with tongue-in-cheek. My success results from setting guidelines for residing in the present. No "what ifs" or "if onlys" are welcomed. Instead, "now" gains a sufficiency unto itself. I am learning, slowly.

We work five hours a day, split between morning and afternoon. After work this afternoon, one of the monks invites me to watch with him a videotape of the life of a modern Benedictine hermit, Abhishiktananda. He lived much of his adult life in India, trying to find experiential connections between Christianity and Hinduism. My monk friend focuses upon the information that the video provides. I am taken by the sounds. Ocean, river, children, wind—they all make understandable the claim that OM is the sound of all sounds. Everything depends, the hermit says, on awakening to the Source. And how does a Christian hermit in the Himalayas spend his day? "I go to the Ganges, where the river draws all sounds into one. And there I eat my bread, and speak to no one, including myself."

I am coming closer to an answer for the taunting question my friends back in the city keep raising concerning what I am about: "What good do monks and hermits do?" Perhaps their function is to raise that question for the rest of the world. I think of my great-grandparents. They farmed forty acres with a mule, grew barely enough to live on, and never traveled further than twenty miles from home. Their solitary farmhouse, all alone on the Great Plains, was really a hermitage. There were occasional socials, infrequent visitors, and daily living-room worship. They, and hosts of folks like them, functioned as hermit families—or sketes, as they are called. No one ever thinks of asking what good they did, out there by themselves on the Plains. They simply lived the best they knew. In those days, living was sufficient unto itself, for quality still had value. Somehow back then, simply to be remembered by a crudely marked stone at the head of one's grave along the edge of the bleak east pasture was sufficient justification of one's life.

Twenty years ago I discovered a grave while hiking in the Rockies. At its head was an oak board with the hand-carved word, "Karen." At its feet was a mayonnaise jar holding cut wild flowers. It was sufficient. So is it not enough for fifteen monks, or even one hermit, to struggle over a lifetime to be faithful? My answer is not a grudging one, but an envious one. I am being brought to a deep appreciation for those called to spend their years praising God for the gift of each new day, giving away everything that is not needed, practicing hospitality toward all, and praying continuously for the universe and every creature in it. This is what the monk does.

Saturday, September 6

I am sitting in the refectory. It is 4:15 AM. I am sipping my coffee. I am talking to no one. I am content. I am tempted to write the word "happy." What I am beginning to feel in these moments is special, nameless, and fragile. I expect that any moment someone will whisper in my ear that feeling happy in the refectory is not monklike, and that I must stop it, substituting a pained and serious grimace.

Last night was strange. The Great Silence is almost always deliciously silent. But this time it was different. It was "heavy," not "great," the monastery feeling like an abandoned barn rather than a tabernacle. Silence is not soundlessness, but an emptying in order to hear. Last night was soundless. I could hear only emptiness. So it was that this morning one of the monks' mail drawers had become nameless. Is a monk permitted to grieve? Savor and let go, they say. But several times today I am drawn to the mailroom, my questions addressed to the nameless drawer that is now at the bottom location.

The assignment my spiritual director gave me is to develop a daily schedule for living in my hermitage. Then I will try that schedule for twenty-four hours in the monastic hermitage on the ridge. It, too, has a window through which one can "look out upon."

Sunday, September 7

The early hours are forging in me an elemental simplicity. The morning darkness has a tangible silence that one can almost touch. Walking outside, just before dawn, I feel it against my face as mist.

Today I am assigned to be cook. Putting food before the monks is becoming a sacramental act. There is the toasted brown of yellow cheese on coarse homemade rye bread, topped with a circle of sautéed tomato sauce, in a bed of green lettuce.

A visual icon. We have music on Sundays instead of the regular reading. So the entrée today is Vivaldi's Four Seasons, *the fall movement.*

During my after-lunch alone time, the wind is clearly upset. It reels crazily around the buildings, in the pines, through my hair. The sound of such restlessness becomes my Ganges. The only thing like it is an evening rain during Vespers, when the chapel feels as if we are inside a waterfall. Silence and special sounds are strangely related. I am learning how to hear the silence.

Tuesday, September 9

Today is the feast day of Saint Peter Claver. I check him out. He is a seventeenth-century doctor, teacher, and priest, so grieved by slavery that he enters the diseased holds of slave ships as they dock. Prayer for him is for the alleviation of suffering—physical and spiritual. What a contrast with the psalmist at Lauds who wants to be a winner. He is angry with God because he is losing. Then, when he observes that God makes winners "slide to destruction," he is anxious to become a loser, so that he can win! I am becoming clear about the simplicity of being a Christian. It means loving God simply for the sake of loving God.

Wednesday, September 10

This is a fine day, one of autumn warmth and persistent wind. I yearn to pray. It startles me to write that! I have never quite felt like this before. I am surprised that each time I have a *break in my work assignment for the day, I go to the chapel. Even the wind through the windows gifts me, as if it were the sound of an ocean massaging its shore. Ecstasy. Each time I leave, I seem to be inflated with a gentle lightness, gliding along the cloister as if in slow motion.*

Friday, September 12

Over dishwashing, I question my fellow monk splasher about his spirit life. After insisting that each of us must find his own way, he hesitantly shares his favorite spiritual disciplines. "I do a quiet and slow reading of Scripture in my cell, pondering and tasting and listening. Then after Eucharist, I just sit in the chapel, and from my deepest self comes thankfulness." He thinks for a while, and then finishes: "Oh yes, some special evenings I just go to the chapel and 'be.' That's all. Very simple, but it's me." My brothers are mellow, honest, simple folk. Nothing special.

This afternoon a monk invites me to take a walk. Our steps are slow and quiet. The leaves hint of fall. We sit on a log. A hawk soars high. A spider seems too busy for a weekend. We seem to be here for a long time. I'm not sure. Seems that time has taken the day off.

Sunday, September 14

This is the day for beginning my solo in the monastery hermitage. Last night I remembered with apprehension the words of my spiritual director: "You will be surprised by the sounds of the night." An old prayer takes on new urgency: "Lord, protect me from the beasties that go thump in the night." I sense, however, that it will be the ones inside me that will make the most sound.

I promised that my twenty-four hours be open-ended and unscheduled, within a monastic rhythm that is firm enough to inhibit my habitual work patterns. Then I pack, pleased that my adventure is taking on a sense of play. Sunday in the monastery is distinctive. After mass and lunch, each monk wanders off, disappearing into "whatever" or "wherever." And so do I, with a cumbersome canvas bag of supplies perched precariously on the handlebars of an antiquated bike. The quiet woods prepare me, broken only by several of my yelps as a tree deliberately jumps into my path.

I arrive at the hermitage shortly after 1:00 PM, with only the bread somewhat bent out of shape by the journey. The hermitage is simple. There is a screened front porch, with a cistern beneath. The inside is one room, with a stone-floor alcove as chapel. The furnishings are a narrow bed, hot plate, refrigerator, sink, lamp, and desk—with a window overlooking the hills. So, I'm here. What now? Nothing to do. The place is already clean. Cup of coffee? Why not? A chair on the porch? Good idea. Nice breeze, with a goodly supply of birds and sun. One of the monks had slipped me a note "for opening later." Now is later. I open it. It is entitled "Hermit Suggestions for an Intellectual." This is his advice. "Before sleep, go outside and look at the stars. Leave time behind. Learn to be without. No searching allowed. No answers. No questions. Touch the Mystery. Taste the grandeur. Feel the Breath. We love you." Amen!

I keep expecting some figure to come waving down the path, with a problem for me to solve, or recalling a responsibility I have betrayed. None come. How rare, to be where only three persons in this whole world know where you are, and they are pledged not to tell. Some persons might be terrorized by that thought. I want it to be a gift.

Here I sit. I have not been here long. Or have I? It does not take long to realize that to be able to exist in a hermitage where I am nobody necessitates trusting that, in spite of everying, I am loved. The desert is where such trust is tested, for to be an unloved hermit would be suicide.

I still do not know exactly what Presence is. I find myself tiptoeing around, opening windows wide, peering out. Strangely it is as though I do not want to miss anything. I go out into the afternoon sounds. They do something deep inside of me. A moment ago I found myself shifting weight from left to right, helping a hawk glide motionlessly in the wind. There is sky everywhere, as if someone has taken off the lid.

At twilight, I am called into a walk. The saplings are beginning their red welcome to winter. Then, as I am returning, I see the hermitage from a new angle. Suddenly I remember. Long ago, I brought a class of students to visit this monastery. It was my first time here, too. On the way back from making concrete blocks with the monks in the valley, one of them drew me aside and asked if I would like to visit "the hermit." I had thought that hermits were long extinct, phased out with the dinosaurs. My curiosity won out. With all the naïveté of a gaping tourist, I followed the monk, scrambling up a steep hill. I now recognize that it was on this very path that we came out, leading to this very hermitage. And as we approached, the hermit came out to greet us. He was a tall, gentle, warm, caring man. "A cup of tea?" He invited us to come in. On his desk, the very one on which I am writing, there was an open New Testament in Greek, a notebook, and a volume by one of the mystics. So here I am, ten years later, in that very hermitage. And on that very desk are my Bible, a notebook, and a book by Saint John of the Cross. I am he! How deviously the Holy Spirit works.

Vespers is a bit strange, at first. I feel sheepish, like being caught talking to myself. The monastery bell bongs, far away. That helps. I keep thinking the word "rehearsal." The liturgy begins to settle in, for its own sake. The final chant of Compline lingers on into sleep. Night sounds, all around, like a "praying without ceasing," for their own sake. It is a quiet insistence, somewhere near D major. I hear the Angelus bell from the monastery tower. Sleep is an embrace.

Monday, September 15

An alarm clock lacks the subtlety of bells, but it is effective. Vigils at 3:30 AM is by candlelight. A fireplace would have been perfect. A pack of coyotes offers the antiphon, something about being alone together. My lectio divina *is by Saint John of the Cross. I struggle with him for two hours, until I doze.*

When I awake, everything is wrong. I slept longer than I should. I wasted valuable time. I'm off my schedule. I've failed again. What a total reversion is happening. I can't even get the door unlocked to go out and greet the dawn. The key won't turn. That hardly matters. Who would want to go out into such a miserable day anyhow? I had expected daybreak to be the advent of a glorious fall. Instead, rain is thumping on the roof, slurping all over the sides. Like a spoiled child, I sit in the chapel alcove and sulk, refusing to light a candle. The most pious euphemism I can give for such behavior is that I am pouting, like a little child. This is clearly not what Jesus had in mind.

In spite of myself, I begin chanting psalms to the rhythm of the rain. It draws me, still chanting, to watch through the window. It seems as if twilight is surrounding the morning. Mist as incense begins rising above the hills, and heavy fog drains into the valleys. Trees become silhouetted on tiny hill islands popping up through the intense whiteness. I put out a tin can to measure the rain. The sounds all around become a purring gentleness, as if I were breathing it in and out. Even the occasional thunder belongs, like an Angelus bouncing off one hill with a response by another.

What a fine day this has become, just right for cozy reading. Time to try Saint John of the Cross. I am open to him. Yet the more I read, the clearer it becomes that this is not a spirituality for me. Central for him is the "dark night of the senses," through which one attains union with the Beloved in ecstasy. I understand his insistence on self-denial and the importance of "loneliness and dereliction," where through "aridity" comes the joy of emptiness, purging the desire to control and possess. That makes sense, fueled by the yearning to serve God alone, for its own sake. His goal is as appealing as it is overstated: "Fires flash in the abyss of the pure heart whose loneliness becomes alive with the deep lightnings of God."

But his way of getting there is unacceptable. He insists that this goal is attained "in proportion as the breasts of sensuality are dried up." The union he advocates is interior, divorced from senses and feelings. I pause for a long time. Not only does such a goal defy my experience, but it is neither my hope nor even my interest! When I begin reading again, I feel anger rising as he becomes increasingly insistent. The soul must "deprive itself of the pleasure of all that can delight the sense of hearing," forcing that faculty to remain "unoccupied and in darkness." Each sense in turn must be stripped away, for the "habit of rejoicing in natural beauty enslaves the heart." So severe are such temptations, he insists, that few persons can be found who have not been "stupefied and bewildered by this draught of the joy and pleasure of natural grace and beauty."

The very things that I love, he is declaring to be lethal: "If some antidote be not at once taken against this poison   the life of the soul is endangered." Purge every taste for the earth, he declares, for "hatred of the world" increases in proportion to one's love for God. He even warns those entering the desert not to love the sand. And those housed in caves dare not stroke the contours of the rock, or even its moss. Maybe not for John, but I will insist upon it! To be delighted with the earth, he declares, is to remain as a little child. Then, with Jesus, I shall yearn to be that little child. Clarity is coming.

As I keep reading, his denials begin clarifying something deep inside me. In heavy contrast to him, I am beginning to know that my spirituality involves desiring more, not less, feeling more deeply than not at all. I am being called to taste, smell, hear, touch, and see, as never before in my life. His is a spirituality for introverts, and I now know mine as characteristic of extroverts. This is a rare moment, in which I finally acknowledge that I am an intriguing hybrid of flesh and spirit. To choose only one of these, either one, means denying both my Creator and me. Christian revelation centers in the Incarnation. Jesus Christ is the joyous interpenetration of spirit and nature, made for each other. And if flesh is for incarnation, then the whole of creation is for Divine-human covenant.

I now know who I am. My soul thirsts for the spirituality befitting a poet—one inebriated by living. What do I want? Now I know. A carnal spirituality, a fleshly mysticism. This makes sense of the power that the Eucharist had over me in that Colorado monastery, when the chalice seemed to be a valley molded by the mountains. And here, now, it is happening again, even more. The earth itself is becoming a Eucharist, and this tiny hermitage is volunteering to be its chalice. And, best of all, I am ready to wager on it. God is in, and with, and through, and by, and under, and maybe even as the creation. Yes, mine is the spirituality of a little child, standing awestruck in the first snow.

During midmorning prayers, with the mist soft against the windowpane, I make a vow: that I shall live this life of carnal spirituality from now on. I shall settle for mediated Presence. No, I shall glory in it, for it is a spirituality that sacrifices neither God nor earth nor me. Emptiness, then, will be the purging I need in order to be filled. Silence will be a denial in order that I may hear better. The purpose of fasting will not be to atrophy the appetite but to be an aperitif for the banquet. Sitting at this spiritual window, I feel liberated, freed to glory in what I am seeing. Towering pines are playing with the abundant breasts of endless hills, bathing innocently together in the slowly undulating mist.

It is noon now. Intimacy is laying claim to the hermitage. I spy a Sacramentary on the top shelf of the closet. The desk by the window would make a fine altar. The tin can collecting rainwater outside will become both chalice and element. And here, overlooking the Ozark mysteries, I shall have a Eucharist for the whole of creation. My prayers of intercession last over half an hour. After a while, I have to cut them off. They can never end. The mist keeps rising as if incense from wooden thuribles. I drink half of the sanctified water. The other half becomes a gift to a pine seedling struggling between two rocks. The door unlocks easily. I am ready to leave.

Tuesday, September 16

Back at the monastery, I awake this morning with a deep sense of being gifted. The name "God" intertwines freely with thankfulness for things recognized for their own sake: a cello well played, a carefree walk in the rain, a motorcycle ride aimed at a sunset, a friendship that wants nothing, and prayer simply for the sake of praying. I remember as a boy my favorite response to the question "why?" was "just because." I am beginning to live life deeply, "just because." I continue to smile over my first meager success as a hermit.

The psalms at Lauds must have been chosen just for me. "Awake my soul, awake lyre and harp, I will awake the dawn. . . . May your glory shine on earth!" I walk into the mild morning as it blows against my face. The world is a better place today because yesterday a novice hermit baptized a fledgling pine.

A brother expressed sorrow that I had missed his anniversary day yesterday—thirty-five years as a monk. "They gave me a surprise party for lunch. Lasagna, my favorite. No one has ever remembered me like that." There were tears. "I saved some for you in the refrigerator."

A letter arrives today from May Sarton. "Your letter was meaningful because I am recovering from a long illness and a slight stroke. So your phrase 'I seem to learn best by walking into my weakness' hit me where I live. I like to think of my Journal of a Solitude in your hands, and the solitude itself which will be your sweet challenge soon to come." At Vespers I pray aloud for her: "May you the Spirit be gentle with May's soul, that wisdom may continue to be birthed in her through weakness."

Thursday, September 18

As I sit in the refectory with my morning coffee, the oldest of our monks asks if I can identify a quotation for him. "Yes," I reply, "Cardinal Newman wrote that in one of his poems." He is taken aback. I ask why. "Long ago I was told that poetry is not for monks. I had written poems, a whole box full. So I burned them when I entered." "It's okay to write poetry now." "Yes, but I don't tell anyone." He recites one about a wren he heard singing one morning when he was a novice years ago. The more he talks, the closer he comes to joyful laughter. I must believe that God is smiling all the while.

I walk outside into a melancholy of falling leaves. Strangely, I remember that Saint John of the Cross begins where I do: "On a dark night, kindled with yearnings. . . ." My self is never satisfied. And so it should never be, for an infinite longing can never be fully satisfied by a finite anything. But unlike him, it is these very things of the earth that cause me so to ache that life itself radiates as a search for God. And God? So far I only have hints. But what hints they are. Another one graces me as I look full-faced toward the fall sky, watching with envy as a V of geese fly beyond the horizon. I can only watch. Joy is the carnal form of hope. I am happy.

Saturday, September 20

Tomorrow is the day. I will leave for my own hermitage. I spend the day trying to distill the learnings that have emerged from my second crash course in Hermiting 102. I need to be concrete, to take them with me as a down payment against a second failure.

1. My model will be Jesus' own desert experience. My exterior demons are the temptations that society so widely advertises—the three P's of power, prestige, and possessions. The mind of Christ, which shall be my model, emerges as the opposite: abandonment, humility, and vulnerability.

2. Such a reversal of motivation will challenge my inmost dynamic, that of self-justification. The edges of the desert have already exposed the dead-ends of living by my own efforts. Truly to enter will take me more deeply into its emptiness, into a pure longing for grace. I am beginning to know what a grace-saturated life would feel like. It has something to do with unconditional love, followed by a quiet, smiling, gentle OKness simply in being.

3. If any of this does occur, it will be God's doing as gift. What I am called to do is to live as rehearsal, to practice a disciplined life of as if. For this, the Eucharist will be central. May I lift the chalice daily as if filled with rain for a thirsty earth, to be blessed by the hidden God, and returned as manna sufficient to feed God's incarnation everywhere.

4. I must let Mystery enfold me, for I go where I do not know, for reasons that are not clear, seeking that which I know mostly as Absence.

Late this afternoon, someone puts a journal article by my cell door, on the theme of "Desert Spirituality," which I read. I find helpful the contrast between the spirituality of the mountain and that of the desert. The first is experiential, for one does not climb a mountain in order to stay but to find something useful worth taking back to one's daily life. The second, however, is a matter of irrevocable commitment, for one does not enter the desert in order to be fulfilled. Desert spirituality is desperate, beginning at the point of no return where everything is "up for grabs," and one is not free to turn back with fidelity. Simply to endure in the desert is to triumph, with faith simply the commitment to see it through—no matter what.

I become frightened by what I read—phrases such as "no recognizable landmarks," unclarity about who is looking for whom and who started it, of needing to stare down the Mystery, or having only whispers on which to wager against a background of bad bets. I have so little on which to wager, and yet, when I trip over the evil around and in me, falling full face in the mud, there appears a mockingbird overhead, incorporating my curses into a delightful melody.

I find a quotation by Trappist monk Charles Cummings that wraps itself around my soul, so I slip it into my pocket as ballast for the road:

> In the desert we go on serving the God whom we do not see, loving the God whom we do not feel, adoring the God whom we do not understand, and thanking the God who has taken from us everything but God's own self.[4]

The bell for Compline is ringing. I leave in the morning. I am ready.

4

Into The Silence

After having had such a failure in my first attempt at life as a hermit, I am trusting that my second period of formation at the monastery has provided a stronger core by which I may persevere in my second attempt. With the help of my spiritual director and a send-off from the monastic community, I once more enter my hermitage—trembling, but with hope. I am tired of running, even though what awaits is likely to be my "moment, when darkness reigns" (Luke 22:53 NEB). I have chosen the following journal entries that have helped me appropriate what happened during this time.

Sunday, September 21, 1986

The final assignment from my spiritual director was to confirm with him my revised design for a typical day at my hermitage. He listens quietly as I indicate that the seven monastic hours will be my basic framework. I will set aside time for different types of praying, and for journaling, reading, writing, and playing. I will endeavor to make meals sacramentals. I will listen to news on the radio once daily, followed by intercessions for the world. And there must be music. As I share all this, however, it feels as if these ingredients could become just another work list of doing, to be checked off each sunset—with my lamenting that the list that is never finished. Yet he nods approval, adding a splendid rule: "Keep the schedule immovable enough to keep your natural habits restrained, and flexible enough to enable you to be led." Fair enough. We embrace.

This is the morning to leave. To remain at the monastery any longer would be all talk.

Dabs of sunlight sprinkle the awakening hills as I drive away. The trip to my hermitage goes quickly. The morning is glorious. I open the hermitage door. I am home. I have returned. I close the door behind me, with a firm resolve. This hermitage is an open, light, and airy place. Walking through it is like touching the insides of my own soul. I stand in the center of the hermitage, viewing the work of my hands. Not bad for a depression boy who does best in redeeming the throwaways of a wasteful society. I sense how Eucharistic this place is. Every salvaged piece has been lifted up as an offering, blessed, and received back for forming a sacred space.

I remember my uneasiness when I built it. How would I feel when it was finished? Would it have meaning once there was no "doing" needing to be done? Could I simply "be" in it? I find assurance in the fact that when I have been on weekends here, it takes only a few minutes of wind through the cedars for all to be well.

All day long I delight in the familiar: each nail head, the grain of each board, the stupid little building mistakes now funny—it all feeds me, smiling as a friend. For over ten years,

I have been led to this place and to this time. And now I am finally here. Standing at my front window, listening to the murmur of insects examining the last twilight, I no longer feel like a stranger. I can even imagine that I belong.

For Compline, I light a candle for a simple but special liturgy prepared from gleaned quotations worth stuffing into my pockets over the last weeks. I bless my loft with a paraphrase from Rahner: "Blessed are those to whom God chose not to be revealed. They are the most blessed, for the highest perfection of religious existence is to hear the silence of God—and believe." I bless the chapel with my own version: "Faith is the courage to give away my life to the One experienced as the Absence implied by my longing." I bless my desk by the window, using my remembrance of Pascal: "A religion which does not affirm that God is hidden is untrue." But my favorite, from Carl Michalson, I keep for the entrance gate. Beneath a heaven ablaze with stars, I read by flashlight.

> You can ask me, "Well, Michalson, don't we know that there is a God?" We do not! Honest to God, we do not! If [God] is our Father, we do not know him. We love him. Do we know that Jesus is the Son of God and the Lord of our lives? We do not know that, not with that hard kind of knowledge by which we characterize business and science. We do not know it! If [God] is all that, then we are [God's] servants. We do not know [God]. We obey [God]! Don't we know that God raised Jesus from the dead? We do not know that! We are [God's] witnesses; we worship. Do we not know that the church is the body of Christ? We do not know that! If we are its

members, we serve it. Don't we know that the future of history is on God's side? We do not know that, because in history we are pilgrims. We hope. My friends, the Christian message is a proclamation that strikes the ear of the world with the force of a hint! [1]

I have one more hint: that the Jericho road ahead is hot and dusty, rumored to harbor thieves. But I have a new poise. It is as if I have memorized the map in advance.

Monday, September 22

I awake remembering the miserable week I spent here not very long ago, before my intermission with travels. Trying to avoid a repeat performance, I set aside the next two days for entry. So today's agenda is dusting cobwebs, giving proper burial to a rotting mouse, unpacking books, and, of course, making piles. Is this a reversion to doing? It feels different. It is more like creating external order as a preliminary context for shaping the disorder inside. At the moment, it is difficult to imagine this place ever being a desert. The thought of spending months here is delicious. But I am sure this will end soon, for I have had to bring "me" along.

Triggered by the evening news about an escaped convict in the area, I go to bed thinking of The Amityville Horror. As I remember it, a family moves into a house whose former owner was murdered. The book focuses on a supernatural sense of presence in that house, spooking everyone. Here I am, all alone, as the night sounds come from the outside, and strange creaks from within. I have long lamented the absence of Presence. But with goose bumps rising, it just hit me. What if I *really thought that there was Someone in here, in the darkness, watching? I thought of locking the door. That would be absurd. Even if absence is lonely, the thought of presence becomes even more alarming. Now what?*

Tuesday, September 23

I awake with the same uneasiness. Would not a gracious God honor one's need for privacy, refusing to invade the space one needs in order to be? There's a group exercise in which two persons walk slowly toward each other, stopping only when they establish the comfort zone of their relationship. I need to belong, but I might die just as quickly without the solitude of an empty space never to be invaded, not even by God. The two of us will have to walk toward each other soon, very carefully.

At bedtime, I wonder if God's apparent absenteeism, which has bothered me for so long, might be in fact a gift of Presence as loving absence? A psychiatrist once told me of a woman who was incapable of sexual relations. She felt that God was watching. The release occurred when the therapist used an analogy. If she would have no respect for a parent who enjoyed watching her through keyholes, how much more would this be true of God. So she turned a picture of Jesus to the wall, and her sexuality emerged. Could it be, then, that prayer is my invitation, granting God permission to enter a space in which, in some sense, God would not otherwise be? If God limits God's knowledge for the sake of my free doing, would not God limit God's omnipresence for the sake of my free being? Yes, God and I are indeed working on our comfort zone.

Wednesday, September 24

I believe living the monastic schedule here will be possible. The solution is quite creative. Not long ago a friend wrote, asking why the monastic schedule seemed so impossible for me at the hermitage, but so possible for me at the monastery. My answer came quickly—the persistent bells! So in the mail I received the kind of endless tape used in answering machines, on which she had recorded church bells. In the same box came a timer capable of being set to turn on the tape recorder at multiple preset times. And, presto, instant monastery. Thus at 3:15 AM, I have no choice but to go down the circular stairs from the loft to the chapel, and turn off the bells. I am sleepy, but impressed.

Thursday, September 25

Today is a memory day. It is said that a drowning person's life passes before him or her as integral to the process of dying. Something like that is beginning with me. I somehow knew this would happen. To the degree that I am able to put work aside, to that degree am I beginning to be flooded with forgotten memories. All day long it seems as if I am in an editing room, with monitors playing on all sides. I suspect that a bad LSD trip is like being locked in such a room with inferior clips of one's questionable past being stuck on instant replay.

Many of the tapes are beginning to have a common theme. They seem to have been triggered by a dream several nights ago. It was about one of my friends, an older woman, who had put off her call to ministry as long as she could hold out. Long overdue, she finished seminary last spring—only to die the next day. When I awake, the flooding begins. There is the memory of Mother's silk sheets, which she received as a wedding present and then saved for the rest of her life, waiting for the special occasion that never came. There is the remembrance of the bank account into which Dad put spare money for years, saving to take the European trip that death unscheduled. I remember a colleague longing for retirement, only to receive with his first pension check a diagnosis of incurable cancer. This may be why I have avoided silence much of my life—it resembles death. And now the total silence is trapping me with the question: "Do you know anyone who is living life fully, now?"

Friday, September 26

Yesterday's barrage continues to have time as its theme: the shortness of time left. Today's reruns specialize in clay feet sticking out of worn trouser legs. I have hurt people. While, I hope, not intentionally, nonetheless I have hurt them. What were my motives?

The recorded bells sound for Sext. Instead, I turn them off, and wade out into the rain. "I want to be clean." *But the images keep coming. I go back inside and sit on the floor, precisely in the center of the hermitage. Episodes sweep over me: the drive to be seen, to be affirmed, to be someone, to win and never ever be a loser—never again.*

Monday, September 29

I keep saying that I want to lose myself in something or someone. But accompanying that ache is a deep guardedness. When I am vulnerable enough to risk being claimed by another, I begin to feel smothered. Then I get defensive, and my intellect turns feelings into ideas. I feel safe in the world of ideas, for a while. So by afternoon, I render myself safe. It isn't too difficult. I just insist that what I am experiencing is the common human dilemma, calling forth what Tillich calls the "courage to be."

It is evening. I watch as a hawk rides the rain, like a surfer who personally knows the breakers. How fine if some-day I could live that way, without need of compensation beyond the quality of life lived for its own sake. But instead, my restlessness is taking on secret expressions now. There are places and situations emerging from the shadows, only dimly remembered. Awkward birthday parties. Dances without a partner, afraid to ask and afraid of being asked. Award assemblies seen from the balcony. Knowing about an event without being invited. Secondhand knickers that won't stay up. Being chosen last in a pickup game. Damned to wear wire-rimmed glasses from the third grade on. And then there are the hurt eyes, just staring back at me.

The bells just sounded. Vespers is my time for offering up the day into God. It seems best tonight to do it without the set liturgy. I permit the waves of images to continue, choreographed by the antiphon: "I need to atone." Such praying went on and on. This is no wallowing in guilt. Nor is it a desire to undo an unchangeable past. I am reaching out for a reconciled present.

Just as an "Amen" finally prays itself, I recall writing once to a person with whom I had been strained. It was an apology, followed by an invitation. The letter was not returned, nor was it answered. That is all right. I needed only to send it, not to force a response. Tonight feels much like that night when the letter was sent. It is time to acknowledge the way things are, even if it may in some cases be too late.

Tuesday, September 30

The whole day is one of "roving prayer." I sit very still as my imagination moves in and out of rooms, cities, porches, attics, alleys, now beginning the phase of releasing names with faces. This is very hard. I do not move. I feel dirty, like being involved in a wordless confession in the presence of a friend whom I treasure. I can only take so much of this. I do not know when I have been so intense. I want to get out, but the rain keeps driving, echoing my thinking. So I start pacing, at the same tempo as the rain.

It is hours later, maybe even days. It is hard to know. To stop the mental sideshow I need to make something with my hands—anything solid. Tomorrow I will build a wood rack for firewood on the deck, to hold the broken boards I collect from abandoned lots in the inner city. But for the moment, I can only stare out the window, building an imaginary roof against a non-imaginary downpour. I must build something. The life I have is becoming unglued and unnailed.

After supper, the rain stops like a reprieve. I walk down the path to the lake. The woods take on a lemon color, with leaves etched in chartreuse. As I reach the shore, there is a hole in the clouds, torn asunder by a double rainbow. Such a festival is my Compline. And from my bed I look out the window onto the world, handdipped the color of twilight. It is like a hand-written note reading: "Permission to Be."

Wednesday, October 1

Rain begins again about midnight. It rains hard all day. If the animals begin walking two by two, I'm out of here! I listen to the 7:00 AM news daily, followed by intercessions. Today's broadcast centers on serious flood warnings for this area. When I am alone, I am better able to identify with those who suffer. I ache for those in the flood path. There seems to be a direct rela-tion between my growing love of living and my sensitivity to injustice. If life is no big deal, to be deprived of it is no big deal either. But if one is ecstatic about living, to live it is to fight for life, everywhere.

Early rising is no longer a chore. In fact, the dark hours are precious. And my daily Eucharist in solitude has lost its previous feel of make-believe church. The liturgy I use is Catholic, and my authority for being a celebrant is Protestant. Sounds odd, but feels right. Chanting psalms by myself as I pace the floor is no longer weird. But the truth is that this is a very hard day. Day after day I am being reminded that the problem with being alone is having to be alone with me. As the weeks go by, it is less easy to hide. My bombardment by images continues unabated, loosely glued together by self-doubt. Will they never stop? Is human interrelatedness much more than an *intricate web of cross-scarring, of being hurt and hurting, and then reversing the process? I feel unstable. The highs are getting higher, and the lows progressively lower. Is my morality anything more than disdaining in others the temptations eating at me? Maybe I could handle all this if there were only me. But my beginning is someone else's ending, and my ending a beginning for those who follow. We are all stuck with each other, at least to the third and fourth generation.*

All day I pray to keep calm. I am trying to let the internal flood waters take me where they will. I focus on steady breathing, in hopes that my spirit can move more evenly over the troubled waves. Faces are surfacing now, some with smiles giving delight, others with sharp stabs of pain. At times I giggle, while at others my arm rises involuntarily, as if to hide my eyes, or deflect a blow.

Thursday, October 2

I begin this morning to do some intentional editing by discerning recognizable periods in my life. The segment that glares back at me the most is the cellar door labeled "Earliest Childhood." I suspect that much of my life has been spent making sure that door remains locked, and the cries muffled.

By noon, it becomes too much. I need air. Pacing the deck only makes it clearer that I cannot be changed, no matter how hard I try, unless there is release from these wounds haunting my past. Just to rehearse them is to make them even stronger. My strange, repetitive behaviors must have compensatory reasons hidden somewhere down deep. No matter how painful it will be, I must discern what plot they are forcing me to act out, often against my will. No sooner have I confessed this than the convergence of discernments finally comes. Your temptation is to treat others as if they were your mother!

I am frightened. The only direction out is forward. And the logic of forward is to plow deeply enough into the branches of hurts that the intensity of pain will lead in the direction of the taproot. Silence is the most relentless of drivers. If anyone ever asks me what the necessary ingredient is for making a desert out of one's life, I can tell them precisely—the solitude of silence. When robbed of diversion, the haunting follows inevitably. In the editing room I watch for recurrent patterns, received and perpetuated. To do unto others as I would have them do unto me is turning out to have a nasty side effect. It gets lived out as treating others as I have already been treated.

I am thankful for the seven daily offices. Without their witness to the fact that others have successfully traversed the desert, I could get swept away. "May the almighty God grant me a quiet night and a peaceful death. Amen."

Friday, October 3

I awake feeling drained. Yesterday I stood halfway between fright and defensiveness. Today seems to be the advent of vulnerability, as a wavering between immobilizing despair and excitement worn thin by fatigue. So today for hours I have been recording on the back of reused paper everything that memory dares to unearth, considering each period of my life in turn. No value judgments are permitted, only the memory itself. Such *tilling of the soil entails stacking stones as hedgerows. The number of pages is mounting at an alarming pace. The analogy comes to me of digging up rusty tin cans from a meticulously manicured lawn, suffering from shallow topsoil.*

This is severe. But what is harder still is realizing that this identifying is only the beginning. Clearly there must be displacement, a rooting out of the tumors, by reliving those episodes that are functioning as the hinge points of my life—whatever they may turn out to be. I must relive memories in the present, experiencing them as the person I am now. But who am I now? And even more, who and where is the God who will need to walk with me in the cool of the day? Or explain things to me on the road to Emmaus? Or have balm for the Jericho road? If the loneliness of my childhood is to be transformed, there is no other way. It is one thing to stand again as that skinny kid by the fenced-in corner of the kindergarten playground. It will be quite another thing if the revisit would be wrapped in the assurance that nothing can separate me "from the love of God in Christ Jesus our Lord" (Rom. 8:39).

Saturday, October 4

I am on the barbed edge of fright all day. For help, I search in my library for Dennis and Matthew Linn's Healing of Memories.[2] At least the title is apt. But they make it sound easier than it is. They call it exchanging my feelings for myself for God's feelings about me. But what if accepting God's acceptance means flying in the full face of what I have been forged for over fifty years to think of me? That would mean doing something like rebreaking a crooked bone in order to straighten it. No, it involves even more, a more for which I am uncertain that I am ready.

I know the name for what I need. Grace. But what needs to happen this time is for me to accept myself, as Scripture says, not in general but in the intensely personal way in which God accepts me—as unconditionally loved, just as I am. Healing depends on standing naked before God, open handed, having dropped all the tidbits of self-acclaim, so that I am able to receive humbly what I really need.

I am beginning to sense the incredible difference this could make for me. How astonishing it would be if I no longer need to prove myself. What a solace it would be to be able to see myself honestly, compassionately, redemptively, creatively, probably in that order. No wonder Saint Paul calls grace the gift of love by a gracious God. There is no way that I can just decide to feel differently. That would only be a pretense, saying everything is OK when it isn't. How can I as an untrusting self be brought to trust that God truly wants to heal me—not only me, but also all those whom I have hurt, and those who have hurt me?

I am certain that any healing for which I can hope will not be once and for all. In fact, I suspect that it will entail a life lived as a disciplined rehearsal forging new eyes. Any new orientation must be sufficiently practiced if I am to be able to wage war daily against the resurgence of the life I have been rehearsing for almost a lifetime.

Sunday, October 5

This painful process of discernment has been going on now for well over a week, or maybe a lifetime. I am worn down, poked by numerous one-way signs pointing toward outright confession. To surrender my root memories will require restitution, as much as is possible. I am no alcoholic, but what is happening makes me feel that I am addicted to something, wandering in a desert with twelve sand dunes landscaped by Alcoholics Anonymous. Their program begins with a guttural admission: that I am powerless to change my undesirable and thus undesired behavior. Then, by relying on a "Greater Power," one has the courage and support to begin an inventory of one's whole life—confessing, making amends, and receiving forgiveness, all the while keeping the process ongoing by helping others to do the same. Is this to be my roadmap as a fledgling Christian?

By Compline time, I have had enough. Where is the equivalent of AA's recovering-companion whom I can call when I need him? He is in a hermitage on a hill, without a phone. Still, there is no going back. But can I at least take a seventh-inning stretch? Why not? So I take one, using the remaining daylight hours to fashion the wood shed that I already imagined into preliminary being. With more pounding than necessary, the shed takes recognizable shape out of nothing. I finish just as the persistent rain sets in for an all-night stand.

Monday, October 6

I know this will be a desperate day. I must not permit a 3:30 AM rising to be an excuse for postponement. But actually these early morning rhythms are becoming friendly. I no longer rise with electric lights but with a solitary candle. In this dark intimacy I am being strengthened to face head-on what awaits me. And what that may be is hidden somewhere in these pages piled everywhere, secretly describing the baggage of a lifetime. A few things to be done are obvious. The first is a letter I need to send to my ex-wife. Time for rearguing the past is long gone— all the stuff about who started what or why or if. Such issues are now out of bounds. It is over. She is not on trial. I am. Damn but this is hard. No excuses, no explanations, no qualifications, no defensiveness.

What then follows are details in which I take responsibility concretely for my actions, and thus my life. When I finish the letter, I am sweating. I must only write one now. I fight the urge to write them all, to get it done! But that would not be reliving the past, supported by the Spirit that knows the corners of kindergarten playgrounds.

Even with just this one letter written, I seem released to go deeper into my memory bank, into previously forgotten episodes. In the middle of such emotional thrashing, the phone rings. Few persons have this number. It is one of my closest friends, from whom I was once alienated. Our reconciliation occurred ten years ago in San Diego. He had taken the initiative: "Come on out; it's time we worked it out." I went, and we did. But on our final night together, sometime after midnight, he finally said it.

"Paul, you have to forgive your mother. That's the only way in which you will ever know peace." My Compline that night had been a stomping off to bed with refusal and anger. At 7:00 AM the next morning, my Lauds consisted of a phone call. It was my uncle. *"Brace yourself."* *"Dad?"* I had readied myself for that, knowing that he had cancer. *"No, your mom. She's dead!"* Totally unexpected. Even her death was problematic for me.

Simply recalling that phone call is like reexperiencing a deadly weight around my neck. With pain I remember the letter from her that I had in my pocket, unopened all the way to San Diego. I did not want to be lectured to any more. But now that she was dead, I opened it and read. Her last words were like poisoned arrows, the last ones that I would ever hear from her: *"I have often wondered where we went so wrong with you! Love, Mother."* Root memories? I cannot go much deeper than that.

Today's voice on the telephone in my hermitage is that same San Diego friend. Ironically, he is making a pilgrimage down the East Coast into his own past. He sold his business and bought a camper. Then come the words: *"I guess I'm entering the desert, too, but on wheels. I have to put it all together if I am to live well my remaining years."* Then his request: *"Can I come see you in several days?"* *"Yes,"* I said, immediately realizing that I am not ready for that, not at all.

I hang up. I feel frantic. This interruption could abort all that is happening, for I have barely begun the catharsis. I go outside where I will be less likely to suffocate. *"He'll ask me, 'Have you forgiven your mother?'"* There, I have said it! My mind rolls back to when I tried to forgive her. With deep sadness, I acknowledge to myself the letter I wrote to her after she died—and then tried to forget. It was my spiritual director's suggestion: "You need to write her a letter. Bury it on her grave."

By midafternoon I mount the courage to find a copy of that letter. I know just where it is. I wrote it in the Pittsburgh airport, awaiting the last shuttle plane out, returning to the coal-mining town on the side of a mountain by a sulfur creek—a place I once cared to call home. I reread it. Now, with difficulty, I force myself to recopy parts of it into my journal—those parts that resurrect the most pain.

Dear Mother,

I'm coming home. I can imagine how we would greet if you were still alive. It would be a putdown. I can write the script. Paul, your beard looks terrible. Or, are those the only shoes you own? How often I tried to be gracious, and say the right things, but you could hook me so easily. Just by looking at me, I felt defensive. Then you would quiz me on vocational issues. Did you get a raise? Does the seminary president like you? When will your next book be published? Why did you ever move into that terrible section of town? How are the children doing, given all you put them through? Yes, that's it. Everything is "doing" for you, pushing me for all the success stories, with a few digs about the miracle of how well the kids actually did turn out, given my divorce.

Mom! I'm a success. I've got it all. Director of Doctoral Studies and all that stuff. Mom, I'm super-responsible!

I've done everything right! Yes, Mom, you can be proud of me. Please, you can be!!!

Be proud, Mom! I tried. I've been driven to try, all the way to the top. You taught me well. So well that I can't turn that drive off. Even on my "day off," if I don't perform I'm not worth anything—to you, and thus to me. Even if I do work my tail off, it is never enough, never.

Dad was a failure, too. You told me so. He had cancer. You hid twenty radiation treatments from me, so that no one would know. "Everything is fine," you lied to me, until I caught on. But, Mom, you died a failure, too. Guess we all will.

We lived in self-deception. I kept playing the guessing game of what would please you, just as you were driven to do with your own father—unto the third and fourth generations, Scripture says. You dutifully gave yourself to your husband, and to me, so much so that the only life you had was the one lived vicariously through us. When dad was "failing" (your word for dying) and I had already "failed" (your word for divorce and social justice radicalness), this was your opportunity to be a selfless martyr. But you couldn't. If you were nothing without us in life, our failure meant your dying. So you starved yourself to death. You really died of suicide. Mom, I'm beginning to understand us.

I want to be fair. You were "good" to me. You were the one who tucked me in bed, read me moralistic stories from a book about a perfect little boy named Edward.

You took me on walks. In fact, I was always with you. Even on Saturdays, when I was little, you let me take a nap on daddy's side, after he left for work. The irony, Mom, is that I became utterly dependent on you, as you were on me. The worst year of my life was when I was four and a half. You pulled me up the hill in a wagon to my first day in kindergarten. Then you left me. You left me! That was the first time I had been around kids. You left me. The teacher waved my hand at you out the window. I cried, uncontrollably. The terror of abandonment. Without you, I was nothing. And to be accepted by you, I had to try to prove myself by being who you needed me to be, in order for you to prove that you were a good-enough mother for your own father to affirm you. Yes, that was what was going on. A vicious circle defined both our lives.

We were all oblivious to what was going on. And it's too late now. You're dead. But it doesn't matter. Even if you were alive, you and I would be powerless to change anything. We would simply rehearse things, making them hurt, over and over. So here I am, a few minutes from takeoff. I hope that I can really bury you, once and for all. I doubt that you will stay dead. Forgive you? I don't even know what that would mean. But, for the first time, I think I understand you. I'm coming, Mom, and this time I know. Paul

As I read the letter I had written for her grave, I am devastated. I knew far more than I knew that I knew. And I believe I know more now than I knew then.

In the dark wet gloom of this evening, I am certain that the answer I need is theological. *I have never met anyone who is not scarred by the past, and at the same time desirous of avoiding the desert. As I sit here, staring out through the window at nothing, I am ready to gamble that the unfulfilled need I have of the mother who has scarred me is deeply related to the primal craving in each person's soul.* For both mother and me, the hunger has been for unconditional acceptance, love without strings attached! *I must indeed grieve the unavailability of that parental love I have wanted so much. But it goes even deeper. Not only did she not give it, but in all truth unconditional love is never possible from any human, and certainly not from a mother now dead. That game of nearly fifty years, that dynamic, that dead-end is over. But what I am sensing is that the intensity that emerges from acknowledging that dead-end is disclosing in me a still-deeper craving—for Love of another order.*

It is long past my bedtime. Before my friend arrives, I must face this quandary which has been half a century in the making. I am excited. I am frightened to death.

Tuesday, October 7

Immediately after Vigils at 4:00 AM, I feel ready. My prayer is passionate, requesting that the Spirit be my companion throughout this desert wrestling. Then I spread all over the floor my journaling, my scribbling—everything that represents the years of being "me." Sifting through this mess will be much like turning up the pieces of a puzzle, looking for corners and borders. Hour after hour I work at it, taking no break for fear that I will not have the courage to return to the task. And finally, to my amazement, what I thought would be an incredibly complex endeavor is becoming nakedly clear. The plot within the plot is telling its own story. Root images peer out from beneath life metaphors.

By evening, I tape clean sheets of paper together. As the process keeps defining itself with increasingly broad strokes, I am able to cluster similar images together on the paper. It is like sorting out reds from yellows and blues. Blockages keep opening. Out tumble names, forgotten faces, as if in remembering what is already damning, there is no longer any fear of knowing it all. Episodes take on a vivid multicolor. I can feel the texture of cracked paint on doors I have hesitated for years to open. I smell things with the dank odor of a root cellar. I hesitate at an attic door. The process takes on a momentum all its own, as I watch. But most important of all, I can watch because this time I trust the Spirit to remain comfortingly at my side as companion.

Wednesday, October 8

I work almost all night. It is finished—at least the beginning. The results are in front of me, taped like a worn but trustworthy roadmap. Two powerful images emerge as hubs. It is around these two that everything called my life has tended to cluster, as variations on those two themes. The first root canal to be acknowledged and confessed is my fear of rejection. In living this dread, I have always felt like an orphan, dreading the conclusion that I may not be worth keeping. Illustrations placed around this theme crowd off the paper as if hemorrhaging: skinny body, *only child, depression clothes, wire-rimmed glasses, shyness, the last chosen at games, lonely at recess, slight speech impediment—on and on.*

And there is a second theme. I am physically trembling as I dare record my reexperiencing of it. Every night, after being tucked in bed by Mother, the house would become very quiet. Then I would tiptoe through the creaky length of the upstairs, slide down four steps on my stomach to a landing where I could peer down between the banisters. This nightly liturgy was in order to be certain that my parents were still there, that they had not abandoned me. Then I would return to my room, prop a chair against the attic door, and clutch my teddy until my arms ached. One night was different. I did my nightly ritual. But as I peered down between the banisters, there was no one there. I had always known that some night this would happen, that I would be abandoned, utterly alone! I searched the house.

The name for this second fear? Abandonment. *Its feel is that of being an exile, as if I am not worth remembering.*

Suddenly my memory releases the story of my birth. My birth was a life-and-death struggle with Mother. "I think your son will die, but your wife will be OK." Those were the words told my father sitting in the waiting room. Soon the forecast changed. "No, we will probably lose your wife, but your son will probably make it." And later still, "Maybe both will survive." For a lifetime we both have been struggling with that "maybe." A scar from the forceps is still on my cheeks, marking where I was wrenched into life.

I was told once that when things do not go well, a Jew will say, "What a bad thing to do!" A Roman Catholic will say,

"What an awful person I am!" And a Protestant? "How insignificant I am!" I was born Protestant.

Thursday, October 9

I am working nearly around the clock on this process, fearful of going on, and fearful of stopping. "O Lord, hold my hand." Somewhere around midnight, a second large sheet of paper emerges, identifying what has flowed from these two negative root images in my years of living with them. It does not take long before the sheet names itself: "Coping." The question that keeps pressing in upon me at this point is the one I have been asking myself: "Paul, over these many years, how were you able to deal with the fears emerging from these unmet fears and needs?" Negative answers start coming first. On the one hand, I keep persons at arms' length, so that no one can know who I really am. On the other, I rebel, before others have a chance to leave me. So protected, my accompanying strategy is to work with all the intensity I can muster in order to make sure that I will be of sufficient value to others that they will neither forget nor reject me. I am driven to make myself worth keeping around. There, I've said it—finally.

But the burden has been heavy. To be worthwhile is a constant and overwhelming endeavor. To stop means risking that the floodgates of self-doubt will reopen and bring an onrush of anxiety for one who inwardly knows that he deserves to be rejected and abandoned. Then there is always the one sentence clincher: "I have often wondered where we went so wrong with you." I pray for strength.

It is probably near 2:00 AM when a third sheet begins to come into being, one that marks itself "Compensation." It is at precisely this point that I begin to experience something strangely important. I had been certain that finding anything positive resulting from my hurts would be slim pickings. Yet, ironically, while I came up with two primal hurts, there is an outpouring of positive memories. I need more paper.

Finally, there can no longer be any doubting it: from these very hurts have been forged my fundamental strengths as a human being. *I push myself to be concrete, for this is hard to believe, let alone to accept. Among the attributes I write on the chart are my persistent independence; a compassion for losers; an imagination that dreams things and people into their possibilities; critical thinking that asks "why" everywhere; a social conscience that fights against all whom society would reject and abandon; and a sacramental hunger to lose myself ecstatically.*

I have been in the desert since childhood. But at this moment, simply as I write, I sense that I am coming out on the other side of the desert, tested and affirmed. The power of this appraisal is that it is no longer based on what I do, but on who I am. And if this is so, then there is an erasure occurring deep inside my soul: the need to accomplish in order to be. If this is likewise so, I cannot conceive a more radical conversion.

Can it be that such freedom grants the ability to get in touch fully with my feelings, those that I tend to repress? I can no longer deny it. Joy is what I am feeling—JOY! *Just before sleep overtakes me I pray, "Thank you, God, for permitting me to see myself through your eyes."*

Friday, October 10

With moonlight playing at the edge of my bed, I awake, rising before the instant bells, feeling new and eager. Is "rebirthing" too strong a word? I am determined to see this process through the sea of reeds to the rock on the other shore. It takes me only one cup of coffee before another sheet emerges, this one labeled "Problems." I ask myself what that means. The answer seems that I am to be concerned here with discerning and confessing the sins that keep emerging in my life because my primal needs have not been adequately met. What warning signals have I dismissed? This means looking for leftovers, for I have partly worked my way through this question when I named those from whom I must ask forgiveness and, where possible, make amends.

By noon I can smile, for the last sheet to emerge has a fine name: "Conclusions." Apparently I am nearing some kind of welcomed closure, at least for the time being. The conclusions distill themselves out in naked simplicity, as if the Spirit is a wind blowing across a threshing floor, separating the wheat from the chaff. And as I finger the golden grain that remains, letting it fall as it may, I experience slowly but firmly a peace I have never known before. Does it make sense to say that there is a creative fit to all this redeemed junk?

As I write these words in my journal, may they be received as a prayer. "O Lord, may such peace quietly remain, always." There will be a need, of course, to confess from time to time. But when it happens, may the subsequent recelebration be akin to what I am experiencing now. It would be naïve to believe that these weeks of struggling, in themselves, will be *sufficient to undo a lifetime of coping habits. But this I know. It is a solid beginning for the cure of memories that must be ongoing.*

It is night now. The day has been long. I light a candle, and begin the Eucharist. When it is time to consecrate the elements, I read from my final page of newsprint, the one called Conclusions. It is my meager way of letting go of everything I can, intermingling my pain with the blood of Christ, and my new life with the sacred bread made flesh. I am unprepared for the overflowing of prayer that erupts. It begins as affirmation— of thankfulness for the me that has been accepted, and that I finally like. I really do. I have never been able to say that before.

Then, as a final letting go of everything I can as an offering to God, I write the following sentence, acknowledging in this journal what I have never dared to acknowledge before, even to myself: "I am blessed not to have ended up in a mental hospital."

With these words finally said, the drawbridge to the other side comes down. And unbelievable though it is, at the far edge of the bridge, as it were, I stop and surprise myself with one more confession: "It has been a good life, all in all!"

The Eucharist refuses to end. Instead it draws me into a deep pondering about what may have been at work in all this. And the affirmation to which I am drawn is as simple as it is profound. To experience what I have been experiencing has to be the meaning of Presence. *At its heart,* Presence *is less something to be felt, and more something whose actions are to be recognized after the fact. There is simply no way, short of unspeakable arrogance, that I could have come to all these* reconciling conclusions on my own. *If left to myself, my self-interest would have resisted to the bitter end all inclinations toward becoming vulnerable.* In fact, only in trusting the grounding and embracing Presence can I make the miraculous declaration that I am about to write: "Without having received these primal hurts, the odds are that I would have blindly capitulated to a sanguine and unquestioning life, and by polishing the surface would never have become who I truly am."

My eyes roam over the papers now taped to the walls. I can no longer deny it. I kneel in acknowledgment before the altar table. Reseen now with new eyes, I celebrate my life as having been filled with far more joys and creativities than hurts and regrets. I never knew that before. *I raise the broken bread of pain into God, and am given refreshment in the comingling of blood. For the first time I can affirm at heart's depth Paul's summary of the gospel: "So if anyone is in Christ, there is a new creation: everything old has passed away; see, everything has become new" (2 Cor. 5:17).*

The Eucharist is an awesome event. It turns images upside-down. Turning wine into blood is elementary compared to what the Spirit is transfiguring in me at this very moment. Here, by candlelight, in the center of a Eucharist, in a place unknown, I am being released to remember and re-remember. I laugh wildly.

On and on the Eucharist goes, until I feel that I am glowing in the dark. The things I had thought about myself, things that had converged into a "low self-image" of myself, are now being heartily challenged and replaced. I have often said

*that I would never want to relive any part of my life again. One
time through is more than enough. But at this moment, I freely
and gladly confess:* "I would be excited to relive it all. Living
life to its fullness is self-justifying."

*The blessed Eucharistic elements and my own blessed life
comingle this night, as I thoughtfully and thankfully eat and
drink, more than once. As benediction, I sit outside under the
stars. My mind dips and soars among a host of freed memories,
as connections are born and reborn.*

*Even during a hot bath by candlelight, the delightful kalei-
doscope keeps turning. These past several days I found myself
doodling. I recognize one particular shape now for what it is. It
is an unconscious sketch for a greenhouse addition to the sleeping
loft of this hermitage. With happy tears, I remember asking
Santa Claus for something I always wanted: a toy greenhouse.
I never got it. But I know now that on the far side of the desert,
youthful memories are reemerging as playful invitations. This
hermitage will soon have a greenhouse.*

*Sleep is the Spirit's way of passing the peace, bringing
closure to an extraordinary day.*

Monday, October 13

*My journal has gone empty for several days. In enjoying
the newness of who I am, words seem pointless. There is no
need to do anything with what has happened to me, or to push
anywhere with what I am feeling. It is what it is, intrinsically
whole, self-authenticating, with no need of explanation or
defense. All that matters is living it. But there is one question*

that lurks in the quiet corner moments. Will this last? Since I did not cause it, its longevity is not in my hands, and thus even to try to make it last would be a sad idolatry.

The persistent rain is bringing the lake to record flood heights. I walk along the new shoreline, feeling sorrow for the trees, shivering to their necks in icy waters.

Tuesday, October 14

The heavy clouds overhead for weeks finally have holes poked in them, like worn sheets on the edge of being thrown away. Yet even in the rain everything is greener than I have ever remembered it. My friend has been here for the past several days. Then this morning, as we sit across from each other after breakfast, without any prior hint, he quietly asks, "Do you mind if I leave?" Within fifteen minutes he has done just that. Previously I would have searched for what I had done wrong. No longer. We had done with mellowness what needed to be done. He sensed that somehow I was different. He gloried in that, and apparently had no need of explanation. He knew that I had finally been able to do what he knew I had to do, before I knew it. It is over. Thus our whole time together was his, and so we hiked around the edges of his soul. And when it was time, the discernment came. His search, which he once thought was vocational, and then intellectual, turned out in fact to be quite spiritual. So he is gone now, equipped with abundant paper and pencils, on his way to an ashram.

Thursday, October 16

Each day, the water continues to rise, lapping against the shore like a nervous snare drum. Today it becomes ominous, creeping slowly toward the hermitage. And while a month or so ago I might have been on the near edge of frantic, feeling intensely the need to do something, today I experience it as an invitation to play. Out into the rain I dash, scandalously unclothed, the rain streaming down my face, and mud splashing up my legs. I am a child again—or maybe for the first time. Fond gifts of remembrance flow back: the crunch of first snows, the smell of burning fall leaves, the anticipation of Christmas Eve. For the first time in my life, I find myself filing them in my mind under a very new label: "Experiences of God."

Part of clearing away the clutter of yesteryear has been writing more atonement letters. I have faithfully written one each day for a week now. Each one writes itself, as in turn each tells me when it is time to write. Each letter is as intense as it is difficult—to say things straight out, without shifting blame, without flinching, without hiding behind generality, without pressuring for any response.

Friday, October 17

I am happy. How strange it feels to write these words. But I need to acknowledge it, for even my daily offices are quite different. No longer are they a duty. They are invitations. And at midmorning I pray Terce on the lake shore, to the chant of wild ducks. Lunch is on the deck, shared with Rosie. She is my stone-carved mystic friend living under a slight roof beside the deck. *She was rescued for a dollar from an Indiana garage sale. I used to envy her stability. No longer. I have my own.*

5

🌿 Presence of the Absent God

The following entries from my original nine-month journal seem to select themselves as distilling well the final two months at my hermitage—as I attempt to appropriate what happened. After my crucial breakthrough, there emerges a delightful stillness as the center of my daily living, focused by the emergence of a new understanding of God. The hermitage feels increasingly like the home I never had. And, above all, the Absence of a presence becomes the Presence of an absence.

In mid-December, I begin the transition from my hermitage solitude to a resumption of my former extroverted life of inner-city living and teaching. This chapter ends with the delight of two Christmases, culminating my experience in both monastery and hermitage, which together with the city form the places of my love.

Sunday, October 19, 1986

It appears that my time now will be with less internal fanfare or staggering uneasiness. At least that is my ongoing prayer—to live by honing finely the sense of having come home. How many new births does a person need—or can handle?

Above all, I feel a profound sense of thankfulness. This, along with Eucharist as the focus of thankfulness, is the basso continuo of my daily living.

Several years ago a blind pastor friend gave me a foot-high walnut cross. Even though it was nicely done, I kept it in a drawer, unable to relate to it. I brought it with me to the hermitage for one last try. Today, for no particular reason, I get it out. It sits on the desk with me. It continues to sit there all day. Nothing. Then, just minutes before sunset, I am drawn to go outside. I do not remember making any decisions. I just gather some odd-shaped twigs, and an acorn with cap intact. Back inside, it takes only glue and ten minutes. The polished cross becomes a crude crucifix. Now I understand. Empty crosses know too much—or too little. Tomorrow I shall hang my new crucifix over the altar in my chapel.

Wednesday, October 22

Today makes conscious to me the certainty that my call into solitude must always go hand-in-hand with my call into social justice. There can be no other way for me. To fall in love with living, living fully as a friend of God, leaves no choice but to struggle against everyone and everything that denies or contorts the fullness of life for any and all. Relatedly, my own intense struggle with the reality of rejection and abandonment is making me more sensitive to those whom society has so treated. Thus I was excited to receive a letter from a seminary colleague who recently resigned his professorship, gave away his money and possessions, and moved to Nicaragua in order to live with the poor. I save his letter so as to savor it this evening by candlelight. I read it slowly. My feelings begin turning in the opposite direction from what I had anticipated. What I increasingly feel is a deep sadness and disappointment. Instead of sharing with me his own life and hopes, he starts at the very beginning by passing a stringent critique on my life. "In so far as your life does not represent a full participation in poverty, it is a deception." He questions as well even the idea of my taking a sabbatical. "Its motive is to strengthen you for service to the system!"

A month ago I might have been rocked by such rejection. Not now. I am truly and madly in love with life and living. And what follows inevitably for me is that my foe is whoever and whatever deprives others of the fullness of such joyful living. My yearning prayer, then, is that the opportunity for such love must be made possible for every living thing. Instead of wanting to hear about my pilgrimage and where my sabbatical is leading me, my friend wants me to substitute his pilgrimage for mine. I am sorry that he needs that kind of affirmation. I blow out the candle.

Long have I preferred Luke's version of what Matthew calls the Sermon on the Mount: "Blessed are you who are poor" (Luke 6:20). But now, as my eyes revel in the Milky Way smiling through the side window, Matthew's version takes on new import: "Blessed are the poor in spirit." Jesus knows the real test for that kind of poverty. It is the degree to which one is able to do what one has to do without letting your left hand know what your right hand is about (see Matt. 6:3). My friend is following Luke. But duty will burn him out and turn him in upon himself, unless he follows Matthew into the desert. Then any questioning he might want to share with me will have the power of integrity, for then he will be a comrade.

Very late into the night, I feel my way to the spiral staircase that rises to the sleeping loft. T. S. Eliot wrote about getting one's own land in order as London Bridge is falling down. To do this, physical poverty entails letting go of my props. Spiritual poverty entails going behind society's cardboard scenery to the hollow icons of its own construction. It is important that we be brothers. Through the window by my bed, a full moon is rising like a communion wafer, its reflected light baptizing the horizon with mystery.

Thursday, October 23

I am discovering how many of the small things that I used to make serious are becoming invitations to play. Without a sense of humor and playfulness, life becomes treacherous. This afternoon I am playing with a pan of Jell-O with floating bananas on top. It is like herding kittens.

Little things keep happening, deliciously, moment by moment. I am living in awe that both the highs and the lows are serendipitous gifts. Before the beginning of my spiritual conversion in the monastery's hermitage, baptized by mist and rain, much of my life was a strenuous work-oriented skirmish to arrive with Dorothy at the Emerald City. Now I keep finding one-way signs on the desert road pointing back toward Kansas, where I can see each corn field as emerald—for the first time.

Friday, October 24

At dawn it happens. I knew it would. I am sitting outside, hot coffee in hand, as brace against the fall chill. All seems to be at peace. But as I look out over the lake, colored gold by a rising sun, it suddenly dawns on me that I am in a cauldron of death. Unsuspecting insects are being gobbled alive by jumping fish, while overhead the gliding gulls in turn make periodic plunges upon unsuspecting fish. Whether it is hawks spying the landscape for rodents, or the spider beside me weaving a web for entrapment, everything that lives is doing so at the expense of something else. Pain, fright, suffering, and death—these are woven into the fabric of creation. Suddenly the issue is no longer just that of a skinny little child in a creaky Appalachian house peering nightly between the banisters to make sure his parents have not left him— yet. At this present moment, that kind of abandonment looks tame in comparison with the kind of abandonment I am feeling now as an adult—living in a carnivorous cosmos. I shiver as I look down at the rocks, fully expecting a coiled copperhead at any moment. How can I have anything to do with a God who designs and blesses such a painful and deadly arrangement? Must I conclude that the game of winners and losers that I find so offensive in today's society is actually the way God has organized the very universe, even down to the interplay of lichens and rocks?

And yet, even before this grim conclusion can sink into my soul, I feel my whole being reaching out for the sun. To feel its gentle touch on my face seems almost enough, for I am like a plant starved for light. Egyptians called the sun God. I belong, and yet I do not. The God-issue must be addressed soon.

Saturday, October 25

I am surprised that I am surprised, but today another response comes to one of my atonement letters. It is eleven pages of sharing and updating, regrets and joys. It reestablishes a sense of closeness, with hope for new beginnings.

Sunday, October 26

Today is my Sabbath. I permit myself the joy of sleeping late. Then, in due time, I savor hot coffee to the aroma of bacon, fried potatoes, and scrambled eggs. I arrange a concert entitled "Music for a Rain Day." It begins with Bach and Mozart, just for me. Then Grieg and Dvorak for stretching, since I do not care much for either. And a delightful Handel piece, "Sonata for Oboe and Continuo," brings the benediction to overflowing.

It is now late afternoon. The sound is one I have never heard before. This chirping, swirling sound of sheer energy becomes an advent, as starlings alight on the cedars surrounding the hermitage. There are at least a hundred, bordering in my imagination on the billions. I carefully slip outside. I quietly walk beneath them, humorously acknowledging the risk. This restless murmuring sound envelops everything, in all directions. In awe, I stand there for at least five minutes, as if on tiptoes, listening to nature's OM. Then, as though by a conductor's baton, they lift off together, the sheer energy merging in an audible pulse of rushing air. Then all is still, very still. This is a vintage Sabbath.

Tuesday, October 28

Today I remember that I brought with me a box full of old journals, published articles, and clippings that have been dusty companions through the years. I must have guessed, or probably hoped, that here in the hermitage a new beginning would free me to wade through this clutter of the past. An intentionally lean spirit life suggests eliminating all that does not contribute to a lean present. As I begin sorting, I am surprised and delighted by how much I am looking forward to doing this. What an amazing contrast this is to the sense of dread over the past that I experienced just a month ago.

It is evening now. At fireside against a fall chill, I reflect on what I have found. Above all, there are hints throughout my journals that I had not recognized at the time. It is like reading my journal backwards from the present toward the past. Come to think about it, that is the same process that the Israelites found themselves doing. After the fact, they struggle to discern the depth of the plot they have been living. What emerges for them is a clarity so profound that they name it revelation. Safe around campfires on the other side and beyond, they tell and retell as Exodus the story of the strange windy weather by the Red Sea. As Kierkegaard puts it, "Life must be lived forward, but understood backwards." And now, around my own fire, in retelling myself the story, I too am able to recognize the primal movement whose doing is not my own. Memories whose meaning I missed in the living of them are coming together now, as if they are an intentional preparation for my present liberation. Israel's conclusion is a name: Yahweh. For them, the abstract term God has to be transcended, for the God of their experience merits a proper name. Such a process must be what providence is about, with Presence being a retroactive hunch. It makes sense. Now a second question quickly follows. What is God's name for me?

Wednesday, October 29

Over breakfast, I begin to see that the God question must share center stage with another crucial question—that of motivation. My early morning reading in the desert fathers and mothers makes clear that their motivation for striving to be saints is in order to escape the pains of hell later. But I am haunted by the need to transcend any such personal motivation. If one's preference for good over evil is motivated by a calculated payoff, is there any good in such "goodness"?

By evening I have to face the unavoidable conclusion. All religious practices motivated by the hope of reward differ from atheism only in trading present pleasure for an investment in deferred receiving. If the primary rule of the game of life is called reward, it makes little difference whether one chooses a religious stadium or a secular one in which to play.

This intriguing line of thought keeps annoying me all day. But just as I am settling down for a long winter's nap, a fascinating thought decides to keep me awake. Perhaps Christianity at its heart is wonderfully useless.

Thursday, October 30

As I sit by the lake watching the sun show off its final wares, last night's thought continues with me. What I am doing right now is totally useless, for the sun will set very nicely without my orchestration. It always did, it always will—with or without me. If I make the Christ event my model, then living an incarnate life is what I need to be about. This means living each moment to its fullness, for its own sake, as gift. And since Jesus Christ is also the model for God, then incarnation is the clue to understanding God as well. As an early Christian theologian put it, the person fully alive is the glory of God. I suggest a corollary. God fully alive is the glory of humankind. So put, I can understand John Calvin's insistence that the primary end of being human is to glorify God and to enjoy that God forever. If so, then the primary end of God is to enjoy and glorify the cosmos in the process of becoming All in all.

The Trinity can help me understand the richness of such a God. God as Creator is the ground of all that is, calling us to be cocreators. As Redeemer, God is immersed with us in suffering, as the crucified one enabling our reconciliation. And as the Holy Spirit, God is the throbbing, primal Presence in and with and under and as the sacred Energy racing through all that is, driving and luring everything toward consummation.

So understood, the healing process in which I am immersed must involve more than a purgation of the past for the sake of the present. If not, my illicit passion for power, prestige, and possessions simply shifts its focus to being the motivation for doing "spiritual" things. Such a shift, in turn, makes my situation worse off than before, for now I operate out of self-deception, hiding me from myself. Thus, even praying that God's justice might prevail may be nothing more than costumed jealousy, calling on God to get back at successful persons for having what I really want but have not been able to get. In fact, even the desire for sainthood, understood as guaranteeing a heavenly ticket in the box seat section, may be little more than my sour grapes for having personally failed on the human plane. In delving into the complexity of human motivations, I tremble at the deviousness of my own behavior. As Reinhold Niebuhr insists, my uniqueness as a human is my ability for self-transcendence, which provides the possibility of creativity, freedom, and conscience. And yet this uniqueness to which I am called can also be my undoing. Just thinking about all this is wearying and frightening.

Friday, October 31

Today, my first attempt at sainthood is a disaster. Even now, I do not wish to write about it. I am moving a chair in out of the rain. How it gets there I do not know. But as I close the door, I gasp. A snake has wiggled inside the door, and is now at my feet. Snakes always frighten me. It is probably a small snake, but at this electric moment it is gigantic. It is only slightly helpful to remember that I had no thought of doing violence to it/him/her. In fact, I remember saying, "This isn't a good place for you to be, and even less good for me if you disagree." The snake is probably cold, moving slower than my startled brain. I guide it back outside with the record cover of Mozart's Mass in

C Minor. *Yet once outside, it just stays by the door, apparently contemplating hibernation right under my threshold.*

Struck suddenly by the image of it sliding into an invisibility that will haunt me every time I open the door, I reach for a nearby shovel. I hit it. Its white mouth gapes open, gasping. I hit it again. And again. I kill it. I feel terrible. I bury it quickly. But the image remains. I feel feelings I have seldom felt before. I keep rehearsing in my imagination what happened. Reviewing what alternatives I might have had hardly helps. It is a fine snake as snakes go, with sleek black glistening lines. I was frightened. I killed it. I am tempted to dig it up. I have no idea why. I am sitting outside on the deck, in a downpour, stunned.

It is hours later. I want to believe that what is still gnawing on my insides has its good side. It doesn't work. It occurs to me that the reason why this event is draining me is that my life in the desert is making violence foreign and unacceptable. Throughout the night, I ask for forgiveness.

Saturday, November 1

Today I read about how a desert saint reacted to his having had his cell invaded. He helped the thieves pack up his possessions, running after them when he found that they had forgotten something. But I killed the snake. I was afraid.

Today is the feast day of Teresa of Avila. I find her very helpful in my pilgrimage. In spite of her ecstatic experiences of God, she insists that they are only special gifts given as consolation to the few. Thus in no way should they be permitted to function as a foundation for one's spirituality. I must let this sink into me, deeply—even write it indelibly on my soul, once and for all. It puts a new light on the lament that I often make that I have never had a direct experience of God. Here is Teresa, not only saying that this is of no consequence, but insisting, as did Jesus, that "blessed are those who have not seen and yet have come to believe" (John 20:29). With or without such experience, spirit life is grounded in faith and faith alone. At its heart, faith is a persistent gambling on the God whom Jesus trusted even in the full face of uncertainty. Or put even better, I trust in the One who trusted in God. When I forget this, then it is that I begin to feel the absence of God, accusing myself of having no spirituality at all.

Yesterday's news indicated that it would take from sixty to ninety days for this flood-control lake to recede to normal. That means death for some of the fine old trees along the shore, now wading. I have some personal good-byes to say to these friends.

Sunday, November 2

The autumn sun paints the forest the special color of old age. My elderly neighbor comes over to enjoy it with me. Delightfully I discover how changed I am becoming in regard to the little things. Formerly my tendency would have been to view the visit as a distraction from my doing. But now, "sitting a spell" ranks high on the list, next to a quiet evening by fireside, having kind words for a clerk, and making soup.

What I am about to write I never thought I would—or could. "If I had my life to live over again, I would choose for it to happen much as it has. From the vantage of this special *moment in this sacred place, I can finally claim: it is a good life, all in all.*"

Monday, November 3

Today my reading from the Old Testament evokes a fascination with the Jerusalem Temple. There is something sacred about citadels of mystery, such as the Holy of Holies, where only one priest can enter yearly, chosen by lots. I feel this intrigue when standing in front of the cloister door of the monastery. This is the place where in former days a monk bid farewell to his family, returning pictures and personal memory objects, never to reemerge alive. This relates to the veiled tabernacle in every Roman Catholic Church, the curtain torn in two. Its interior is publicly visible on Good Friday, when the door is left wide open, for the Mystery has been crucified.

As a Protestant, I welcomed Harvey Cox's Secular City, in which he celebrated the fact that all mysteries are reducible to problems that modernity is well on the way to solving. This year is teaching me that such a loss of mystery is as tragic as it is fatal. Something indispensable dies when sanctuary is only a name for the place in which a congregation meets. Something indispensable is lost when sacrifice is no longer a useful term for understanding the difference between altar and table. Something indispensable is forfeited when leftover communion grape juice has no enigma to it that would give one pause to pour it down the toilet, or have the janitor vacuum the crumbs all along the communion rail.

Tuesday, November 4

Today is the day I have been avoiding. Of this I am clear: Without Presence as my ongoing companion, I could never have worked my way through the desert to the conversion regarding my past. Yet that seems to be mostly an inference drawn from the quality of the result. Is that enough? In terms of actual experience, my thinking is muddled, for I have not been able to distinguish an Absence of presence from the Presence of absence. Over and over again I am brought to realize how much this ambiguity resides in having no viable image of God. But a few things I do know. Somehow any viable image must correlate my healing with the mother I never quite had. In addition, whatever image is birthed, it must emerge with my eyes wide open to the threads of suffering and death woven through the entire fabric of existence. And finally, whatever direction I am taken, may I never forget the terrified shrieks of a mouse I once saw being swallowed alive by a contented snake. With Jeremiah, I wish to "lay charges against you [God] . . . Let me put my case to you" (Jer. 12:1).

Today's crisis in God imagery begins in earnest, with early morning readings from the desert saints. The theme that distressed me before becomes exposed even more clearly here. Their motivations for relating with God are clearly rooted in fear, guilt, punishment, renunciation, and postponed reward. Thus Abba Elias says: "I fear three things: the moment when my soul leaves my body; when I shall appear before God; and when the sentence will be given." Such a God I find downright offensive, and the life that follows from such belief is nothing less than abusive.

The parameters of my struggle are becoming clearer. I cannot love a God who creates a world with violence as its heart, a creation in which everything eats something else only to be eaten in return. Totally intolerable is a God who wills death to anyone or anything. I feel diffused anger most of the day.

I am now able to state my quandary. My most promising clue, one I will not give up, is the joy I am experiencing—in and around and with and since my conversion. Not to believe in God is no longer remotely possible. Instead, and here I think I am getting close, the primal experience with which I have been gifted through healing opens out into an ecstatic relationship to the earth, indeed, to the cosmos. Deeply within the soul, my soul and the soul of the cosmos, a gifted Presence is relating.

Wednesday, November 5

It is 4:00 AM. I am writing by candlelight. Just a step or two outside the hermitage door, with my head turned upward, there it is—the star-spangled universe. Of all the sciences in which I try to keep current, it is astronomy that most fascinates me. Each day, it seems, there are incredible disclosures, whether by the Hubble telescope, missile probes, or computer simulation. There is no particular issue that intrigues me. It is the wholesale view that I find incredible. The very image of a light-year boggles my mind, let alone speaking of billions of galaxies flung across billions of light-years of infinite space, the expansion of which is accelerating. This little earth that I wish to call home has the feel of an abandoned dot in the backwaters of an unknown galaxy, lost somewhere in endless space. I need to come inside.

So here I sit, cross-legged on that dot, in a small hermitage, before a very tiny candle. *And what I experience is a
strong convergence of my own life and the life of the earth—as
a paroxysm of appalling aloneness. I can taste it. The banisters
through which I peered as a child are one with those through
which I stare as an adult—for whether the arena is house or
cosmos, my apprehensiveness is the abandonment of not
knowing whether there is Anyone there.*

Thursday, November 6

*I recall when in graduate school I encountered the Bible
seriously for the first time. The insight that was so invaluable for
me then has somehow been shelved. The image of the new
heaven and the new earth was so intellectually primal for me
then, for it was capable of drawing together the important
strands of Scripture in a promised crescendo. So this morning I
turn to Revelation again, chapter 21, to see if it can ignite what
long ago made all the difference. I slowly read it, again, and
then again. How much I have forgotten. Why? I think it
resides in the contrast between an intellectual conclusion and a
faith commitment at soul's depth.*

*I am not prepared, however, for how deeply this recovered
image sinks into me this time. I read it as nothing less than the
promise of that fullness for which the earth in all its parts now
groans, as if in the travail of childbirth. And this Divine promise,
in turn, flows back redemptively over the whole of history, as
means intersects with end.*

I know now what has been happening to me, and I never understood. The issue is not so much that of Divine absence after all. The nightmare is of a God whom I would prefer to forget, or at least enthusiastically neglect. And that nightmare, as it were, is no other than my childhood God, refined by my philosophical and theological studies, into an image of God as the Absolute. *Yet, in spite of Augustine, Aquinas, and a host of other Christian thinkers, this Absolute is not the biblical God. The Absolute is unchanging, unfeeling, removed from time in an inaccessible Eternity, absolutely perfect and complete, and thus inconceivable by the human mind. Over against all this is the compassionate, gentle, loving, affirming, disclosing, intimate, healing Presence that I now know.*

This is the moment for which I have been waiting. It is a moment that I somehow knew would come. Standing over against this humanly devised superstructure called God, modeled after the Greeks far more than the Hebrews, is a vision that wells up from the inside out. I am readied by my pilgrimage finally to receive the biblical God of the Christ event. This God is the Incarnate One, present on the inside of the ongoingness of everything that exists—creating, struggling, moving, luring, coaxing, pleading, judging, loving, forgiving, thrashing. But for what end? That is the question. The answer is a promise that is to be trusted and lived: that every tear shall be wiped from our eyes, and death shall be no more. Yes! Appalachia, Yale, this tiny hermitage, and me. All one. This promised vision, in the end, has little to do with conceivability and thus the struggle for evidence. It is a matter of trust as a way of living. Here comes the Mystery—that the God who paints the heavens with an inconceivably large brush is the one who a month ago quietly embraced me with whispered affections.

Can it be that the absence that has nagged me for half a century is not so much an absent God as an absent mother? And can it be that the God against whom I keep rebelling is the one with the appearance of a parent who manipulates in order to get her way? If so, then as the Spirit and I work through my relationship with my mother, unknowingly I am also being freed to reclaim scriptural imagery as applying profoundly to my own personal life. Indeed, in me "the former things have passed away," because there is a God who promises to "make all things new." No longer am I dealing with an inaccessible Eternity that relates to me only by rendering the cosmos already complete. Against all this I must live as protest. What is emerging is a strong remembrance of the conflict I had with Saint John of the Cross in the monastic hermitage, when he would not even let me touch the moss in the cave. Or there was the desert father who declared that the wind rustling the tall autumn grass is a distraction from one's spirituality. No, I am as certain as I have ever been about anything. In dealing with God I am dealing with time, our time, our history—and thus God's. Incarnation is God's promise to be a committed participant with us in our living, our imagining, our dreaming, and our yearning.

As I become increasingly open in this fashion, imagery flows: of a Divine-human love affair, a holy city, an adorned bride, a new heaven and earth, a quencher of thirst, and a feeder of the hungry. The One who paints with light-years is the One who wipes away tears and dies my death, being, as well, an accomplished portrait painter.

I understand far better now why monasticism has laid such a hold on me. In spite of the times when as monks we stray from our better motivations, monks are intent upon living as if the Christian vision is already so! There, I have it. The solution to the God-image issue for me is to understand that at soul's depth the real question is what it means to live faithfully. *In spite of my wanting to experience God, I should have been moving in the opposite direction. The believer as hero is the one who* wagers in spite of experience to the contrary. *Faith is not a conclusion, or a pious experience, or an assent to doctrines or propositions. The goal is* pure *faith: gambling one's whole life, for its own sake, on a vision and never to receive either reward or gift.*

I am finding two primary criteria for such pure faith. The first is motivation: believing for its own sake rather than as a means to something else. The second is intent: the commitment to persevere, to endure in faith, even in the face of what might appear to be ongoing crucifixions. On the one hand, then, we are confronted with a demand to "choose this day whom you will serve" (Josh. 24:15). On the other side, at the base of faith's conviction, is the humility to acknowledge that "you did not choose me but I chose you" (John 15:16). Paul expresses it as a paradox: "Work out your own salvation with fear and trembling; for it is God who is at work in you, enabling you both to will and to work for his good pleasure" (Phil. 2:12–13). Only when God works and wills in us, are we able to will and to work within ourselves.

Friday, November 7

At Lauds, my thankfulness is for yesterday's gift of illumination. It undergirds well my pilgrimage thus far. My case for God's objective existence is the joyously subjective inference from my own personal restoration. Healing is faith, and faith is healing. *Scripture puts this well in the story of the blind man cured by Jesus on the Sabbath. In response to the harassment of religious leaders as to who healed him, he finally responds in frustration. My response is one with his: "One thing I do know, that though I was blind, now I see" (John 9:25). From this subjective fact, the restored man draws his own inference: "Here is an astonishing thing! . . . If this man were not from God, he could do nothing" (vv. 30, 33).*

The sun fondles my face. The touch of God? I sense that I have been given a firm foundation for faith. Yet I also sense that the God problem is only half resolved. I think I can pose the remaining question for me: Can I trust that the Divine Companionship in my personal healing is identical with a God who is the Divine Combatant—whose drama in this mind-boggling cosmos is the conflict of Being with nonbeing, promising victory? As a serious Christian, what I deeply need is a metaphor or image with the power to lay claim to both sides of this desperate mystery. The phrase "unruly gentleness" comes to mind for no apparent reason. I am convinced of this: that Christian heroism consists of belief and will in dedication to a vision.

After Compline, as I am entering the Great Silence, one thing seems clear. Known or unknown, my life has been a search for that kind of God.

Saturday, November 8

I awake with the thought that the metaphor that works for my hermit spiritual director in the tarpaper shack is that of Presence, visually symbolized by the Tabernacle implanted in his wall. And my working metaphor? It has not yet finished emerging, but when it does, the dynamic of my heart will merge with the poetry of my head. I have been changed, that is clear; but my head does not yet know how to get current with the experience.

This evening I walk under the tapestry of stars to the sweet smell of cedar and the fresh crunch of acorns. The image of a cannibal universe is fading away. Instead, in the midst of such beauty, smacking of majesty, I feel a silent whisper: "You are home." Embraced, kissed, floating, loved, free to dance toward the North Star. The word gift erupts in my mind. I am gifted by all that is, and by my presence shall I not gift with yearning and with love all that is and shall be? I belong— accepted, adopted, and promised.

The second word that emerges is "accept." When I was a boy, the Scripture often quoted to me was that it is more blessed to give than to receive. And so I have lived my life, gladly giving to those in need, but not being able to receive gifts, either from myself or from others. But here, amidst the swirling stars, I am not even asked to accept. I am plunged into beauty and peace to the point that refusal is not even entertainable.

I come inside, build a fire, and feel led to turn to John's powerful portrait of the resurrected Jesus in the garden. Mary Magdalene does not recognize him, not until one thing happens.

She is called by name: "Mary." Suddenly I recognize how often this type of exchange occurs at key points in the Gospels. "Martha, Martha." "Peter, Peter." Is it possible, indeed can it not be, that my healing is what Scripture means as being called by name? "Paul!" "Yes!" However the image of God finally settles out for me, at its center must be the One who names sparrows and numbers hairs on each head—and calls by name a little hermit in a tiny hermitage (see Luke 12:7).

I recall a passage from Hebrews. "Faith is the assurance of things hoped for, the conviction of things not seen" (Heb. 11:1). I turn to that passage again. Interestingly, after naming many of the great scriptural heroes and heroines, the author gives this appraisal: "These all died in faith, not having received what was promised." They are "strangers and exiles," "seeking a homeland," but were only able to see "what was promised" sufficiently to have "greeted it from afar" (see Heb. 11:13–15 RSV). Yes, to salute the promise from afar, never having received what was promised. Yes, that is pure faith. To believe not because of, but in spite of. Faith, then, is totally removed from reward, unless one regards as gifts such matters as mocking, scourging, chains, imprisonment, being stoned and sawn—resulting in being destitute, afflicted, and ill-treated, as the Christian wanders alone through deserts and mountains (Heb. 11:36–38 RSV). The bottom line of faith is this: we are "those who through faith and patience inherit the promises" (Heb. 6:12 RSV). And the telling factor has to do with motivation, of a pure faith emerging from "the thoughts and intentions of the heart" (Heb. 4:12 RSV). And the conclusion from all this? Faith means trusting the One "whose promise is faithful"

(Heb. 10:23 RSV). I think I am close, once I am clearer about the vision that is promised. All I know for sure at this moment is that I am absurdly happy.

Sunday, November 9

What I previously thought was the question of questions—namely, God's existence—is no longer an issue. If there is a God, I trust God's promises by acting as if they are already in motion. And here is the missing piece that I have found. Even if there is no God, the only way to protest against the absurdity of a Godless universe is to act as if there were one. Thus if the absurdity is that we are capable of loving but the universe is not, my protest to cosmic lovelessness is to love widely and deeply until my dying breath. If the absurdity of the universe is that it is drenched in death and dying, then my protest is to affirm life and fight death at every juncture. And when death inevitably reaches out for me, may I be found making death's task harder by playing leapfrog over the fresh grave. And just before my eyes close, in that moment may I have just enough time to laugh in death's face. Not to act in this defiant fashion would be to affirm suffering and death as the way things should be. In so doing, I would be death's accomplice.

This, then, is my resolution. Objectively speaking, whether there is a God or not, I shall act out of the belief that God is my healing companion. And if it turns out that there is no God, my life shall be a rebellion against a godless universe. In either case, my actions will be identical. Either way, what matters is courage in the face of one's honest wager. Indeed, faith is belief and will, in dedication to a vision.

Tuesday, November 11

At sunrise I walk to my favorite spot, the outcropping of high rock protruding out over the lake. It seems that the birds and the fish, even the wind, halt their busyness. Everything is stopped, holding its breath, standing on tiptoe—as if they are in suspense over what I will do. During the walk I came to some clarity, that what I will do is somehow what I have to do. I feel the weight of the gamble that I must make this morning, for it must be all or nothing. Again Jesus' words arise as the center-piece: "Blessed are those who have not seen and yet have come to believe" (John 20:29). I am ready. With a great blue heron perched on a nearby stump as my witness, I make my promise, my covenant, and my gamble:

"I shall live as if the incarnate, crucified, resurrected, and ascended God gloriously exists, and thus is the pattern for life's meaning. I shall do this by trusting the Jesus who trusted that it is so; and even if we are both wrong, we shall have been faithful companions in protesting together the Divine nonexistence."

The issue that I had previously felt to be so important—the distinction between the absent Presence and the present Absence—is an unnecessary distinction after all. It is both and neither. Either way, I now know how I should live, and why. Since I have lived much of my life as a functional atheist, then certainly I can live the rest of it as a functional theist.

As I settle back to feel the sun, I rest in the peace of having made my life's choice. Yet as soon as I confess this, I know better. This choice has chosen me, with perseverance sufficient to outlast my long quandary. How wonderful the promise Jesus makes regarding the future: No one will take your joy from you. In that day you shall ask me nothing" (John 16:23 KJV). No more questions! I will pray every day at sunrise that this shall be so.

At evening Eucharist, the Scripture is Jesus' teaching concerning the two debtors who owe a contrasting amount of money. Jesus asks, "Which of them will love him more?" (Luke 7:42). I know firsthand—I do, for God has given me back my life. I lift the chalice toward the sacred Darkness, vowing that my life shall somehow provide a name for God, and perhaps a face.

Thursday, November 13

I arise even before the bells, spiritually poised yet only partially satisfied. It makes sense to understand faith as the ultimate gamble. Even if it is in the face of all evidence to the contrary, my gamble as a Christian is that some night my God will be there— and that even now, I shall live the assumption that I am not alone.

Yet still eluding me is a viable image for the God on whom I am wagering. It will hardly do if God is simply watching the cosmic show, or just makes guest appearances, or even is only a companion in my healing. At sunrise, I deliberately walk down to sit by the lake. The only God image that I can ever consider is one that permits me to watch open-eyed the carnage that even now is going on right before my eyes—the slaughter that I have come to call the "feeding frenzy." Fish, hawks, fox, everything is on the prowl to find someone to devour. I force myself to keep staring, even as the "No" keeps rises from soul's depth. The conundrum is kicking at my soul's door. How on earth can I embrace a God who has designed a world in which everything that exists reaches out to kill whatever is to its advantage? Theists are amazed by the fact that anything exists. I am amazed that anything is left.

Friday, November 14

I spend today rehearsing the alternative images for God that I can imagine, from old lecture notes to the outer edges of my imagination. My healing has been sufficient to give substance to my gamble that God exists. It is the who that keeps moving in and out of focus. The God-images that I have been taught suggest either too much or too little. On the one hand, the transcendent, all-knowing God borders on the charge of sadism or indifference. On the other, the God immanent within evolution and history drowns in demonry or impotence. Either way, both images of God fail to evoke my respect. At least my head and my heart agree here. Fyodor Dostoyevsky's novels are classics in exploring these two options: "What are we to do without God"—the issue of meaning, for which I feel some closure, and "What are we to do with God"—the problem of evil, which I have yet to resolve.

By evening there seems to be only one possibility left for me. It is an image that I have rationally entertained before, but its reemergence now needs to be tested by the healing that I have been experiencing. The image is that of reversing the traditional Christian understanding of God as Triune. This orthodox understanding centers in the image of God as Father—meaning a self-conscious, willing, wise, all-powerful, and all-knowing Being, who designs and creates the world. The first pair of humans disobeyed, and so God redesigns the whole world into its present "fallen" condition as punishment for this original sin. Then God, acting as "Son," bridges the alienated distance between Divine and human. As the final stage, this God as Spirit, "proceeding from the Father and the Son" as the Pentecostal gift, pushes and lures the cosmos toward its end. Then there will occur a final judgment by the Father who through the Son has planned and known from the beginning how it would turn out. This understanding of the Trinity makes my dilemma clear. Any God who is self-conscious from the beginning cannot escape being ultimately responsible for the bloody design and texture of the whole process of the universe. *And by what stretch of insanity can one have love for a God whose anger against the original two persons results in punishment by redesigning creation into a bloodthirsty universe, marinated in death?*

Expressed even more painfully, how can the God who is my intimate companion in the healing process ever be reconciled with this traditional understanding God? My sympathies go out to Marcion, declared a heretic in 144, for believing in two Gods. The Creator God of the Old Testament functions on the basis of an eye for an eye and a tooth for a tooth. Then, says Marcion, Jesus discloses another God, one who was previously unknown: the God of mercy. Therefore the Christian must reject the violent and angry God of the Old Testament, for the sake of the God that Paul knew: the God of love. This is a dualistic way of dealing with evil.

But what if I reverse the traditional understanding of the Trinity? What if I begin with God as the restless Spirit portrayed in the beginning of Genesis, moving longingly and creatively over the face of the nothingness which is "without form and void"? And what if this Sacred Restlessness as Spirit lures a creation forth from without and thrusts it forward from within, being the ongoing, driving dynamic within all of nature. To name this Spirit Holy is to believe that the whole cosmic procession is a Divine pilgrimage. God as redeemer, then, is the disclosure of that incarnate God within history as the Divine-human process moving toward mutual self-consciousness. God's emergence from the beginning on, then, is as inchoate consciousness, developing through incarnation in all things, thrashing about to become in time the fully self-conscious God acclaimed by Christianity.

Through this reversal, then, God is not responsible for designing the whole cosmos, creating it in fullness at some beginning point, only in anger to lace it with suffering and death. Instead, the image that is emerging for me is that of creation as the emergence of being from nonbeing. This image applies not only to the emerging creation but equally well for God-in-the-Making. These two journeys, Divine and human, interpenetrate at each point along the way. The traditional motifs that can identify this ongoing interaction, then, are creation, incarnation, resurrection, and ascension. The connection is finally made:

My own desert purgation is a participation in the cosmic purgation that is God. *This idea of pilgrimage as a primary analogy for God ignites my imagination. The Divine emergence is the cosmic struggle with nonbeing through suffering and death, brought to the fullness of resolution. This understanding is simply another way of affirming the vision of the new heaven and the new earth, the image that has attracted me for nearly fifty years: God's promise is for history's consummation. This vision begins as dream, blossoms as promise, and is being resolved as consummation. Through this portrait of the reverse Trinity, my own personal healing intertwines with the Divine promise of the consummate healing of the world. This consummation, in turn, becomes one with God's becoming All-in-all. The psalm at Vespers tonight hints of this connection of self, God, and cosmos:*

> God heals the brokenhearted,
> God binds up all their wounds.
> God fixes the number of the stars;
> God calls each one by its name.
> Ps. 147:3–4 paraphrase

I am very tired. Pondering is hard work. And yet I feel gifted by what is happening. Climbing the spiral stairs into the darkness of my loft feels like acting out this new image of God as emergence. The stairs mount up to a window. Tonight I open it wide, into an infinity of spiraling stars. All of this unbelievable drama is the agony and ecstasy of the Divine birth pangs. And creation is God's desert experience.

Monday, November 17

Not wanting to wander far from the Christian base that has been my anchor throughout this desert experience, my lectio divina *for the past several days has been an immersion in Scripture passages that give affirmation and enfleshment to my emerging image of God. After Vigils under the stars, and now pondering by candlelight, I make some jottings of various Scripture passages to see what emerges.*

God is the Spirit "crying out in every spirit," making intercessions through all of creation "with sighs too deep for words." Prayer is that "inward groaning," as each speck of life struggles eagerly to be "set free from bondage to decay." The pervading hope is that "the present suffering is not worth comparing with the glory to be." Foretastes of this glory come through living life fully under promise, destined for "citizenship in a New Jerusalem." The Christian's faith-style, then, is life lived as if there shall be no "mourning nor crying nor pain anymore, for the former things are passing away." The vision consummates with the image of a banquet where all shall eat at the cosmic Eucharist, celebrating "the wedding feast of the bride and the lamb." All shall contribute from their talents, picking fruit from "the tree of life" whose "leaves are for the healing of the nations," in order that "there shall no more be anything accursed."

I am thankful for this first attempt. It bears witness to me that biblical language can describe quite well this vision that is emerging poetically in my imagination. I recall months ago, when in the monastic hermitage, I hoisted a tin can filled with "the water of life without price," from which "none shall thirst again." It made sense then, and it makes even more sense now, of how God is becoming the fully conscious One. It is through the hungry, the thirsty, the naked, the stranger, and the prisoner like me that this is becoming so, for it is through "the least of these" that it is truly being "done unto" God. No matter the process by which we humans have emerged, it is only through living for others rather than self that the becoming of God as God shall be consummated.

Thus God's cosmic desert has a plot, one whose macrocosm parallels the microcosm of my own healing. This is micromanagement at its best. The Spirit that groans "in travail" in my damaged soul is one with the Spirit groaning through all of creation, as God becoming the healed "All in all."

Wednesday, November 19

On this Sabbath, feelings and thoughts and hands and sun and feet and leaves are getting childishly tangled, as I live out this new image of God taking birth inside me. Shuffling my feet through crisp leaves, imitating a hawk gliding the breeze overhead, I finally understand that this earth is functioning for me as a novel, inviting mutual discernment. My task is no longer that of poking around in God's sock drawer to see if there might be some forgotten notes that can help me unearth God's self-conscious plan. Instead, I am being called to discern the meaning of the whole from within, as co-interpreter with God. Our calling together is to discern the nature of the plot as *it emerges in the process of being written. Journaling is my favorite imitation of this dynamic. Rather than thinking things through to a conclusion and then recording it as a diary, journal writing for me has been the very process by which I discover what is truly happening. So with God's creating.* Consequently, the idea that the Christian is to obey God's will or God's law needs to give way to a very different image—that of being faithful to God's yearnings, as God aches in each thing for the wholeness of all things.

Thursday, November 20

These past several days have been glorious fall days, with swan songs from the remaining gold and red leaves. Correlatively, the rhythm of my days and nights has settled into a sustaining mellowness. The seven daily offices continue to be my framework, with three periods of scheduled contemplation: at dawn, after lunch in the sun, and, my favorite, after Eucharist in the evening, as I become drowsy with the world. As I self-consciously live this primal God-metaphor, a host of other metaphors keep emerging as supplements. I have been reading the book of Revelation again, very slowly. The best imagery is that which is capable of being sung. Next to silence, that which comes nearest to expressing the inexpressible mystery is music.

After Compline, I connect my stereo, filled with Mozart, to a long extension cord plugged into a receptacle beside my bed in the loft. Only as I am going over sleep's far edge do I pull the plug.

Friday, November 21

At the grocery store today I become fascinated by the mystery of eyes. With several persons our eyes connect, and a smile spontaneously surfaces. It is as if the Spirit in me is greeting the Spirit in them as friend. Walking tonight by moonlight, I have the same feeling. It is becoming increasingly easy, almost natural, to image the Spirit as roaming the cedar forest, glorying in its freshness, inviting my friendship.

The hermitage is my friend, simply in being a hermitage. I play with moon shadows on the wrinkles of my bedspread. Their color is one of life's finest mysteries. This is one of those rare nights when things seem so clear—it is a moment as if on tiptoe. I just sit here, the pillow at my back, with a quiet and gentle smile of okayness. I want nothing more than the simple faithfulness of a well-tempered soul.

Sunday, November 23

The image of God as reverse Trinity continues to excite me. Perhaps the reason why the predawn darkness has been so special is that it is pregnant in expectancy. This morning I simply wait for two hours in that darkness, and what slowly comes to birth feels like the Trinitarian disclosure—mystery, followed by order, and finally the dramatic outburst of dawn. I experiment with what it might mean to live this. My imagination ignites with the image of God as the inner and outer edge of everything, yearning from the inside out and luring from the outside in. God is at my fingertips, as well as where breath touches lungs, and where smell conjoins flowers with me. It is exciting to think of living life as if the birthing of God is occurring through the birthing of me—and through everything and everyone, both positively and negatively. So understood, ethics means translating into action the beckonings of the Divine yearning.

My daily Eucharist this evening is more intense than usual. I think it is because liturgy and cosmology are merging. At communion, I take the chalice outside and elevate it as high as I can reach. "Through Him, with Him, and in Him, in the unity of the Holy Spirit, all glory and honor is yours, Almighty Father, forever and ever." Then I drink from the chalice with gusto, throwing back my head. My eyes feast upon the flesh of green cedar limbs pressing against the bosom of an infinitely blue sky. Then I thump and crunch through the thick leaves, with somersaults of laughter. I am being set free to act as if my yearnings for God are the flip side of God's cravings for the fullness of consciousness through me.

Monday, November 24

Everything today is play. I am acquiring a taste for life lived fully and shamelessly for its own sake. At twilight, the woods turn noisy. I shall blame it on three ducks in the cove. I quack. So do they. After that, nonsense makes most sense.

Eucharist tonight is a supper by candlelight. The chalice is a fancy dinner goblet, complete with linen napkin. As I eat, sleep is wrapping the heritage like a soft blanket. The Scripture for Vespers echoes my image of God as the One who is above all and through all and in all, joining and knitting together every joint, upbuilding the whole of creation by uniting all of it in love. Long into the evening, I watch as the Milky Way makes its nightly sweep.

Tuesday, November 25

At dawn, the fog squeezes things so tightly that they drip. The three young ducks in the cove are practicing landings. The sun swirls its fingers through the vapor, adding pink to peach and then to a blue wash. It takes so little to be happy. In this morning's Scripture, Isaiah identifies what this "little" is. We need nothing more than to live under one's vine with one's own fig tree, drinking from one's own cistern. This seems so simple, yet I am convinced that without the desert experience it is impossible for persons just to sit in the morning sun, joyous simply in being one with the creation and its Creator. The God of my childhood specialized in morality: a legislator of rights and wrongs, rewards and punishments. My God now specializes in aesthetics: a Creator of imagination, birthing beauty, delight, and fascination.

The brilliance of autumn is giving way to the earth colors of winter's coming. For as far as I can see, under the trees beyond the cedar grove lies a carpet of tan and brown leaves, splattered occasionally with a dash of orange and scarlet. I have fallen fatally in love.

Thursday, November 27

Today is the one our culture calls Thanksgiving. It is one of two days on which the monks violate their vegetarian commitment. After trying such faithful possibilities as carrots roasted on a stick over a campfire at our traditional Fourth of July picnic, hotdogs were unanimously declared to be a forgivable sin. Likewise, after trying to stuff every known vegetable, the second exception is a Thanksgiving turkey. This feast is the one time when both neighbors and conversation are permitted in the refectory. Yet I am not missing that Thanksgiving event as much as I thought. The reason seems to be that I no longer need one special day for reminding me to be thankful. My days and weeks and months are transpiring to make thanksgiving a year-long feast.

Monday, December 1

I experience today a point where God is at least as close to me as I am to myself. As a result, I understand the mysterious word "soul" as the name for where my longing for God embraces God's longing for me.

This afternoon I try to live self-consciously with such a dynamic. The first characteristic to emerge is that of experiencing the Spirit as straining and pushing from the inside of everything, much as the heart pushes outward, then regroups in order to overflow again. Both God and I thrash about with some blindness as to goal, sometimes with mixed motives and miscalculated efforts. The pushing is sometimes in directions unknown, for

reasons not yet fully conscious, but the longing is for fullness.
"God," said Tagore, "comes, comes, ever comes."

Thursday, December 4

I awake with the words "Yes, yes, ever yes!" Saint Paul
agrees in insisting that with Christ it is always yes. This morn-
ing I became aware of how sensual yesterday's thinking about
God is. I let my imagination go free. After feeling a little guilty
at first, I am quite taken by the thought of sexuality as God's
cosmic sacrament. Paul uses the marriage analogy as his favorite
image for understanding the relationship of Christ and the
Church. Many mystics regard spirituality as the relationship of
lovers. Teenagers, then, groping in the back seat of a TransAm
are a latent liturgy, unconscious of the One for whom they are
really on fire.

No wonder, then, that the Church has been obsessed with
sex. This concern, however, should not lead to the Church's
rejection of sexuality, or restricting sex to procreation, or dis-
couraging its pleasure. The Church needs to disclose sexuality's
essentially spiritual dimension, opening out into the Divine
passion. It should not be surprising, then, that so many highly
spiritual persons have a significant degree of sexual passion.
The deeply sensual nature of some of the finest mystic literature
testifies to this reality. In fact, such mystics as Saint John of the
Cross, in spite of his insistence on the deep night of the senses,
has written poetry that likens the spiritual experience to that of
lover and beloved. In fact, I believe that spirituality and sexuality
may be two sides of a common reality, with physicality and

spirituality being the contrary poles serving as channel markers, linking ecstasy and pained birthing.

Evening is becoming my special, gentle time, as I savor the Eucharist by fireside. This is when my yearning is best stroked by memory and imagination. Tonight is especially one of those times. For the occasion, I locate The Love of God by the medieval mystic Richard Rolle. I remember correctly the character of his writings. The images that flow so naturally from his pages are those of God playing with creation in a primal love affair. Some of his favorite words for describing God's relationship with us are these: shining, sweet, fire, ravished, inflamed, soul, desire, sweetness of hot wine, burning, longing, overcome, comfort, sweet heat, path of love, honey-fed, in labor, unpartable, signs, cries, lover, high, owned, satisfied, music, song, feasting, suffering gladness, melted in love, devoted longing, beauty, wounded, majesty, white heat, swallowed, mad, dying, joy, consoling, free, angelic, sweet-smelling, constant, falling in love, kissing, begging for favors, melt, uncreated light, gifts, consumed, unsatisfied, agony, and rejoicing. Finally, the ecstasy expressed by such imagery crescendos as an ascending to the heavenly gate. And there it is that "the soul has all it could ever want to have, entering boldly the bed-chamber of the everlasting King."[1] Interestingly, Rolle is regarded by most scholars as not providing anything new to the mystic repertoire!

Friday, December 5

*The monastery observes each Friday as Good Friday. At
3:00 PM I walk out to my favorite spot, the rocky crag protruding over the lake. For the Christian, Golgotha is the central
place of history. Here Scripture portrays Jesus as struggling in
agony over the prospect of his death. In this portrayal, we have
a definitive disclosure that the massive suffering of the world is
not God's doing, but God's foe. Jesus as the incarnation of
God reveals once and for all that God, too, is agonizing over
the state of existence. Suffering and death are God's primal
enemies, now and always. Everything depends, then, on
whether Jesus' primal scream of abandonment and rejection on
the cross is also God's cosmic scream. Everything depends on
whether Jesus' sweating of blood in the face of death is God's
torment over death as well. And if the answer is yes to such
questions, then God emerges as midwife, lover, mother, father,
and child, in the bloody birthing of the cosmos, intertwined with
pain and ecstasy. Whitehead's description of our evolving
consciousness describes as well the movement within God: from
Void, through Enemy, to Companion. And in a final disclosure,
the Eucharistic heart surging through creation gains a name.
That name is Jesus.*

*At sunset, I row out onto the lake. I sit. Birds come.
Birds go. Clouds cover the sun. The sun uncovers clouds. Still
I sit. I do not remember ever leaving. But when I become
self-aware, I find myself staring at the crucifix with twigs
hanging in the center of my chapel. And as I sit now in front of
the fireplace, completing the day with a cup of hot chocolate, I*

confess that this tiny hermitage, hiding somewhere in the Ozark hills, is the center of the universe.

I climb the stairs to bed. I am happy simply in being alive. And yet there is sadness, for at my age I am passing from autumn into the winter years of my living. To fall in love is to get hurt, and the deeper I fall in love with creation as God's ongoing gift, the deeper will be my wounds. And so it is for God. But it is a fine choice. And at the end of my life may I be able to say what we as monks say every night: "May the Almighty God grant us a quiet night and a peaceful death." Into your hands, Lord, I commend my spirit.

Sunday, December 7

How amazing it is that the absent God who has been my agony for so many years is turning out to be the ever-present Spirit whom I have been experiencing all my life. My spiritual director images God as Presence, experienced in the feeling of peace. I image God as Becoming, experienced in the creative ache and passion for wholeness. It is strange that the God I seek out beyond the stars turns out to be as well the interiority of everything that exists, pressing outward toward consciousness, and beyond consciousness into the enriched communion of God as self-consciously All in all. Instead of denying any longer that I have ever experienced God, I now claim the possibility of experiencing the dynamism of God anywhere. It is the experience I feel on hearing the first whippoorwill in spring. There, in the throbbing and persistence of its night calling, in defiance of every creature in search of a meal, is the joyous ache of God pleading for recognition as part of the universal yearning.

The more I explore such imagery, the less does the location of God become a geographic question and more a sacramental issue. Liturgy is a rehearsal for seeing—or hearing, if one prefers. David needed 38,000 Levite priests to give God proper praise. That may not be enough.

Thursday, December 11

Yesterday's dawn was choreographed by two great blue herons flying in tandem into the first rays. Today it is a solitary duck gliding through the orange glow of the rising mist, framed by icy limbs, with the only sound being the crunch of frosted grass at my feet. Before my desert time, I kept forgetting (or did I even know?) that all of this goes on every day, just beyond the fingertips of my anxieties.

Over French toast and Mozart, my praying floated into consciousness as a question: "Does this have to end?" When I return to the city in one month, will there be anything in the city capable of luring me the way this place does? There will be rooftops by moonlight, and Sunday morning shadows of fire escapes and banisters on downtown sidewalks. The cemetery across the street from the seminary could promise wooded lunchtimes. I suspect that an urban spirituality will entail opening more windows, telling time by the tempo of the freeways, making faces in store windows, and learning the language of pigeons chanting for shared popcorn.

Friday, December 12

I skim stones far out onto the surface of the frozen lake, playing with the range of hollow sounds. What has been happening to me this year is learning to live the wisdom of Jesus' dictum, the one about taking no thought of the morrow. Previously, all I had was tomorrow, when supposedly I could redeem all my "getting readies." It is clear to me now that without my desert experience, my whole life would have continued on as one perennial preparation—but for what? Death? I now know the secret sought by the wise and guarded by the sphinx. The meaning of life is experienced in being fully alive in each moment as gift.

I remember Zorba the Greek asking a person of ninety why he was planting an almond tree. "I carry on as if I should never die," said the old man. Zorba responded, "I carry on as if I am going to die any minute." I am learning that somehow they are related.

Sunday, December 14

This morning, at the church near my hermitage, I am surprised to hear myself say so easily to a friend, "How's your soul?" On the way home, I ponder about what meaning this word "soul" is gaining for me. It is the name for where God inhabits my solitude. Soul is where others dare not enter except by invitation, and even then, only with washed bare feet. Put another way, it is the interior sacredness of being me. It is where only God can dwell without becoming an in-law who is staying too long. It is where I color my life without attention to keeping within the lines. In a sense, soul is the name for what each person is called upon to create. Thus for some, the soul is superficial, reflecting only the surface nature of life; it is easily emptied out. For others, the soul cannot be emptied, for its deepest edge passes into God. "O God, safeguard that part of You that is entrusted in me to be born as soul."

Tuesday, December 16

I have never known peace to be like this. Yet today one of the psalms at Lauds made me pause: "O how could we sing the song of the Lord on alien soil?" (Ps. 137:4 Grail). The path less traveled that I am taking is rendering me an alien, a misfit. How can I remain faithful when this alien land keeps weighing my singing toward a minor key? By realizing that this faith-style by which I am being claimed is the gift of interior freedom, no matter what the outward circumstances. This is why worship will be so indispensable, for it is the disciplined rehearsal by which I can be so formed that I am able to live faithfully in the belly of the monster. The test of Christian freedom will be the degree to which I am no longer tempted by society's siren lures of power, prestige, and possessions. It is not enough simply for me to give them up as an act of faithfulness. Pure faith has to do with losing even my taste for them. This exhibits the wisdom of having a spiritual director, for in the midst of this alien land, I need someone to sing my song when I forget the words.

In one week, I will go to the monastery for the week of Christmas, and then return here to my hermitage for a second

Christmas of three days with my family. Advent time is when traditionally I write a common letter to friends. Usually I can summarize my year without difficulty. Today it seems almost impossible. How do I capture a year such as the one I have had, without seeming either trite or pompous? This morning I try, without feeling any need to justify my weirdness. I begin with a Kierkegaard quote: "How tragic to die never having lived." With that peg, images begin tumbling out: peach fog at daybreak, steaming coffee by fireside, the purple heart of a freshly cut cedar log, music until happy tears ready me for the delicious tranquility of sleep.

This afternoon I drive half an hour from my hermitage to a larger town that I do not know well, trying my hand at monastic Christmas shopping. I hope I have internalized my hermit lifestyle sufficiently to counter the seduction of loud speakers merging "Silent Night" and "Rudolf" into a medley of Christmas wantings. I am intrigued by how free I feel in a place where I am unknown. I greet clerks and other strangers as if they are potential friends. Shops become invitations to pilgrimage. Through it all, I remain a hermit—a spiritual radical. Exiled as a happy misfit from the madness of buying and selling that is going on all around me, I eat beans and cornbread by a window in the Prospector Café. I look much, and miss little. I may have joined Kierkegaard's spiritual underground, in which the "knight of faith" becomes externally indistinguishable from the crowd, taking delight in everything from pigeons to the latest streetcars. But the deep difference is interior, for I do everything knowing that one is dangling over a depth of 70,000 fathoms, sustained by God alone.

I invite Santa Claus for a coffee break. He smiles through an odd-sized beard, which is no mean trick. He says that he has just come on duty. "Haven't we all?" He understood.

Back at the hermitage, I survey my treasures. With delight I discover that all the gifts for my family are invitations to play. Perhaps equally important, I learn that solitude does not require leaving society. I only need to transcend it.

Thursday, December 18

The morning is still dark as I close the hermitage door behind me. Even though I will be gone to the monastery for only a week, I feel sad in leaving. This place has become my spiritual home. Then, in only two more weeks, I must return to the city and my other life. I quickly put that out of mind, focusing instead on today. I am eager to celebrate this Christmas week with my monastic family. And, as if that is not sufficient, on Christmas afternoon I will return here to my hermitage to be gifted with another Christian celebration, this time with family and friends.

There is something tender about a sleeping world. It seems more trustworthy. And as I drive into the sunrise toward Christmas, I smile at how little it takes to be able to say, "I am living deeply."

Several hours later, I turn from the road delightfully labeled Route OO, into the monastic lane. The morning sun is painting the hills the color of gentle haze, the shade of mystery. There is an outward stability here. Nothing really seems to change, at least not since the sixth century. Folks just get older.

It is here that I first asked the question that made all the difference. It is also here, much later, that I have been brought to the question that has no need of answer.

In my cell is a Christmas card of welcome, and on the door is a note: "You should have come yesterday. We had waffles and popcorn for a snack. We saved some for you." I go looking for them. Both the waffles and the popcorn turn out to be dry, but such caring can turn stones into delicacies. As I finish my unpacking, I discover with pleasure that I have not brought even one book to read. Previously, I would never have gone anywhere so unprepared.

Work assignments are posted on the bulletin board early each morning. Mine is to make the Chapter Room festive. This task has usually been assigned to my monk friend who died this past year. I stop by his grave for any last-minute instructions, and then trot off through a foot of snow in search of a Christmas tree that would please him. My choice is a cedar tree hidden in a neglected corner of the forest. Grinning shamelessly, I pull it to a cherished place in the Chapter Room. Simplicity is the monastic style, so the adornment that chooses itself is white lights and gold balls. Nearby I place a table on which is a vigil candle, a globe of the world, and an old Latin missal open to the words that translate, "This is my body."

In the afternoon, I work with the quietest of the monks, making cedar wreaths for the chapel, hall, and guesthouse. Even Compline has about it a tinge of anticipation.

Saturday, December 20

*Each of us is assigned an Advent book for spiritual read-
ing. Mine is Abhishiktananda's book simply entitled* Prayer.[2]
*He was a Benedictine monk who lived in India as a way of
bridging Christianity and Indian spirituality. During the early
morning hours that are set aside for sacred reading, I become
delighted by what I am reading. He can be understood in such
a way as to confirm much of what I have been discovering. Soul
is his name for God's interior abode. Prayer is the deepest aspi-
ration of our natures, as a spiritual breathing in of the One
within whom we live and move and have our being. The Spirit
pervades each thing to its core, issuing forth as an unquenchable
thirst for the mysterious Source. Once one is able to recognize
this, everything discloses God, calling us to collaborate in the
consummation of the cosmos as Christ's mystical body, moving
time into eternity.*

*Before my assigned work this afternoon, I read that
Abhishiktananda identifies God as being manifested through the
primal appetite of everything. It is this hunger that makes increasingly rich the Whole, drawing into actuality the possibilities of the
Divine life hidden everywhere. Thus whatever the vocation to
which God calls us, prayer works through it as the authentic smile
by which strangers know that they are not alone. The Eucharist,
for him, is the clearest expression of and participation in this
consummation of the microcosm in the macrocosm, adorning the
mystery through which God delights in the creation.*

*This understanding of the Eucharist, to which we both
subscribe, has its test today. A hornet insists on open commu-*

nion *for insects. The celebrant liturgically scoops him from the
chalice, tosses him to the floor, and steps on him, all in one
choreographed motion. But during the Eucharistic Prayer, the
hornet, now under the altar and somewhat lopsided from the
trauma, is able to raise one wing in protest. My attention is
glued to his efforts. "You can do it," I whisper. But during the
Agnus Dei, he gives up his spirit. When it is my turn to receive,
I take the chalice and quietly toast the hornet as a fallen warrior.
Afterward, I give him proper burial beside the Abbot's prize rose
bush.*

Monday, December 22

*Morning coffee at my assigned place in the refectory is in
front of the most wildly decorated Christmas tree imaginable, its
top squashed against the ceiling tiles. The monk in charge
whispers to me his aesthetic principle: "It isn't right until a child
would be delighted." I watch as he continues to bring in his
treasures that he has salvaged all year: strung styrofoam
peanuts, milk-bottle rings, can lids—everything is fair game.
The saintliness of this monk is in his ability to bring forth my
childlikeness.*

Wednesday, December 24

*Tonight will be Christmas Eve. Isaiah at Vigils provides
Advent's climax. "This night you will make your promise
known, and in the morning we will behold your glory." It is
5:00 AM, and again I sit in the refectory, drinking my coffee.*

Apparently unable to wait any longer, the brother brings in a tiny Jesus, reverently wrapped in the sleeve of his cowl. Oh so gently, he places him in the manger under the tree, covering him with a very small blanket. Soon.

Shortly after daybreak, the quiet brother and I install our wreath in the chapel, together with two banners and a handmade crèche. We take gravel from the monastery road and make a path to the manger. It is a fine image. But getting carried away, we crumble styrofoam as imitation snow. The idea is brilliant. The results are disastrous. Static electricity glues the styrofoam crumbs to our clothing, and we become two monastic Frostys. Since we can't win, we join them. We wipe all our clothing onto the wreathes we made, giving them an inspired tinge of snow. This is the first time I have ever heard this monk laugh. Very soon.

My assignment for the rest of the morning is in the kitchen. Several of us pare potatoes, candy the yams, and bake the pumpkin pies. Christmas permeates a monastic kitchen— each pan is in use, begging to be washed and used again. Monks drift in, and monks drift out, finding creative excuses for smelling, and remembering, and anticipating. A benefactor sent a box of "decadents." So, as a finishing touch tomorrow, at each monk's place will be a worldly remembrance. I hope mine will be candy corn.

Much of the beauty of monastic life comes in simplifying things to the necessities. Then the little things gain an uncommon value. A tiny marshmallow bunny for Easter at each of our plates, or a bowl of ice cream on an important feast day, maybe even with chocolate syrup. But what is essential for these nonessentials is a sense of humor, so that even mistakes become a cause for delight. Every Sunday, and on special feast days, we have music rather than having someone read to us. I remember once when, somewhere near seconds on the fried fish, it became clear that the medley of recorded music had not been well previewed. As the wedding march blared out, all eyes turned on a sheepish-looking monk—who quietly smiled and helped himself to more fried potatoes.

Abruptly after lunch on Christmas Eve, all work ceases. With exterior things creatively in place, the task now is that of preparing our own souls. As one monk put it, we need to become mangers for the One yearning to be born. I go to the chapel to play the organ, ostensibly as practice for Midnight Mass. I confess, however, that the real reason is my own spiritual preparation. How better to prepare for incarnation than to lose myself in music. "I danced in the morning when the world began. . . ."

A happy monk am I, at midafternoon bouncing along in a happy blue pickup, down the hill toward the steaming river. As I scramble up an overgrown path, I feel as if my life has been preparation for such a time. I pause near the top for rest, and a friendly hug comes down the path toward me—my former abbot and my present spiritual director, the one instrumental in making my adventure happen. He is my model hermit on the hill. His one-room hermitage is warmed by a glowing wrought iron stove. I had needlessly worried about him. Christmas cards happily adorn the perimeter of his desk. "Can you pick out my favorite?" Yes. It is the one with a child, her eyes hugely open in amazement as she gazes into the crib. With improvised glasses *and the wine I brought, we toast the late-afternoon sun, a deer in the woods, the rolling hills, an errant cloud, and then the whole of creation for good measure. We laugh. Nothing happens. Everything does. We are two little boys trying to live simply and decently with our God. "Time to go if I am to find the path." A Christmas Eve embrace. "Will you be OK all alone on Christmas Eve?" "I won't be alone." Of course not.*

At Vespers, the words finally come. "And now at this close of Advent. . . . " Very, very soon. There is no Compline, for this special night is divided between promise and fulfillment. The promise is announced, and in sleep we await the fulfillment. Half an hour before midnight, the bells ring. I awake, excitedly. The Christ Child will soon be placed in the chapel crèche, and I can make music. We share our simple liturgy with the mountain folk who come to worship with us. The nativity story is read, we have more music than usual, and the incense lingers on like a mist, bathing the little chapel in mystery. This is the night meant for angels and for those reborn to be child-like—those who can stand on tiptoes before the Mystery, with their minds in their hearts.

A second "sacrament" follows our midnight mass, the elements this time being hot chocolate, Christmas cookies, and hugs, as we stand together around the kitchen table. The laughter of our guests sharing the same treat in the guest wing makes for a fine antiphon to our more silent joy. I experience in our gentle smiling a subdued timelessness, wrapped in memories as Presence. When it is time, I go to bed for a second time.

Thursday, December 25—Christmas Day

Drinking coffee early each morning in the refectory is becoming one of my favorite sacramental times. In front of me is this tree, its decorations and under-tree adornments hungrily overflowing toward the four corners of the refectory. Its proud creator has just appeared with one more gift—a new popcorn popper for under the tree. It just occurs to me that he is not finished. He intends to continue making additions for the full twelve days of Christmas! May the child in me never die.

Christmas dinner today is unusual, for we have the delicacy of flounder stuffed with crabmeat. We have a heartfelt prayer on behalf of the friend who sent this fishy gift. Savoring a glass of wine to Bach's Christmas Oratorio is what joy is about. I am ecstatic, for eating together in community I have a clue as to what it might be like to be a holy man. I don't know if I can be one, but for the first time, I really want to. It may take the rest of my life just to become a decent person. At the moment it feels simple—to intend no harm to anyone. In the meantime, there is a little bag of candy corn at my place.

As I open my car door to leave, a monk runs out for a final farewell. "Please come back soon. Your visits are important to us. We are the wounded ones, but we believe we can be healed." There is a rare peace in driving back to my hermitage on unhurried roads on Christmas Day.

Friday, December 26—
Preparing for Quasi Christmas Eve

What a contrast I am living today, as the monastic silence gives way to a three-day Christmas celebration in my hermitage with my extended family. By midnight yesterday, fourteen folks had arrived. Tonight will be our surrogate Christmas Eve, for in a hermitage, time is extremely flexible. Each person has been sent the name of a secret friend for whom one is to make or buy a gift—and to provide invisible tokens of caring while we are together. Something small, made or inexpensive, is to be chosen for each person's red stocking. In addition, each person has a committee assignment, such as being responsible for music, decorations, menu, or liturgy. Mine is to cook the Christmas Eve meal. My improvisation can kindly be called soups: fish, split pea, vegetable, and squash. Actually, I am proud of the results.

This day is a happy concoction of laughter, cookie smells, and "don't peep" wrapping sessions. Increased focusing begins around supper as we ask liturgical questions of each person. These include favorite memories, friends to be remembered, treasured sacramentals, and hopes for our Christmas together and for the year to come. We all pass the exam.

After dishes, there is music: harpsichord, cello, guitars, flute, bells, and pie pans—something for everyone. Applause follows the imaginative suggestion that what just happened resembles a carol. The evening closes gently, with luminarios lighting the path from the hermitage to the lake. As we light them, each of us in turn recalls an important person who has shaped our pilgrimage. I remember Che Guevara. Holding hands with "so great a cloud of witnesses" (Heb. 12:1), we sing "Silent Night" to the abundant stars. The evening's closure is the unique sense of peace that comes from belonging, as a sleepy household stretches out for the night. The desert is blooming.

Saturday, December 27—Quasi Christmas

This second Christmas lasts all day. The first person awake starts the fire. The second breaks bread for the stuffing. The last ones receive a showering of mysterious goodies from their hung red stockings as their wake-up call. A delightfully disorganized breakfast becomes a happening. Time is no issue. Gift-giving lasts for hours—each gift needs to be worn or tried, including a five hundred-piece puzzle. I am pleased with how often social justice issues appear in our presents, liturgies, and conversations—all wrapped in a pervasive playfulness. Finally, with a goodnight hug from one of my daughters, deep words bring tears: "I've been watching you ever since I arrived. There's something different. I just figured it out. You're younger than I have ever known you." As I nestle in my sleeping bag around the last glimmers of a fire, happily in the midst of my five children, I know that my daughter has just provided a benediction for my whole desert adventure.

6

❦ Closure, with Anticipation

I continue to appropriate those nine desert months of monastic hermit life. Looking back now from the vantage point of a year later, I see how well these dual Christmas celebrations distill the faith style of one coming out of the desert on the other end and well on his way to wholeness. Yet there was to be more anguish to come. As I wrote at the beginning of this book, the year that followed the desert experience was far from an easy transition into a previous normality. I stumbled in appropriating it, and thus was thrust into another desert journey all its own. Just as my first venture in entering the hermitage was marked by failure, so too was my urban return. This is why I have had to reenter the hermitage at the conclusion of that city year. This book emerges out of that summer of writing, when I chose and was chosen by entries from my nine-month journal, as I frantically attempted to remake the desert adventure a lasting part of my life.

The journal entries that follow, then, are the ones that offer themselves to me as I come to terms with the final two weeks of closing down my hermitage, preparing to reenter the city. They are wistful entries, for I grow increasingly sad about leaving this place that I have come to love. Yet they express well my efforts at making the transition gracefully and effectively. I realize now, in reliving them, how vital a part of the adventure they are.

Sunday, December 28, 1986

I close the door behind the final loving goodbyes. The hermitage is silent again. Everyone is gone. I slowly gather together the Christmas goodies I received. Candy corn abounds. And now I have a play box. Among its treasures are dominoes, jacks, paddleball, card games, clay, and pickup stixs. When I spy the marbles, cleaning stops. With a throw rug as circle, my memory recalls a warning I have not heard for fifty years: "No hunchies!" Memories used to feel sad. Now they are like Eucharistic prayers, claiming the power to create sacramentals out of unexpected things.

With a passion for restoring my hermitage to simplicity before I leave soon, this afternoon I even cleaned my cupboards. Tucked carefully between the oatmeal and the spaghetti, I found a forgotten note in my own handwriting, dated Christmas, two years ago: "This is written so that I will never forget the time in this kitchen when two of my daughters and I cried, so happy in our relationship that for a moment we experienced a deep fright at the prospect of losing each other." I remember the moment well. We were sharing memories over hot chocolate. As the beauty of things past accumulated, we became wrapped in life's fragility. Tears flowed from a fountain of thankfulness. Terrible pain exists around the edges of loving and being in love, for one has to face the inevitable endings. "Let's go for it anyhow!" one of them said. This has since become our motto for measuring life by intensity. In the midst of our sharing, someone wandered into the kitchen. Sensing the sacred, he eased out. I now realize how much my nine months have been a matter of living out that "vow."

Thursday, January 1, 1987

After intercessions during Lauds, I begin to ponder on what prayer has come to mean for me during these months. My reflections result in two definitions. First, "Prayer is the lifelong project of disciplined formation of the heart, making it second nature to live intensely in the now, in foretaste of the future." Then emerges a second definition: "Prayer entails holding the unredeemed face of the world up to God's promised future, wrestling with God in the agony of the contradictions."

These two definitions seem to intertwine well, much like the spiritual "now" and the prophetic "not yet" are meant to meet and embrace. The future is empty without foretaste, and foretaste is idolatrous without a vision of the yet-to-be. And both rest in a common image of God as functioning at the powerful edge, pushing and luring everything toward its completion, experienced now as foretaste. In the time of my life left, I shall "go for it."

I set aside the next several days to bring closure to my hermit time, for it is almost time to return to the city. I uncover some notes I jotted down a year ago during a conversation with a Benedictine vocational master as he made suggestions for my impending nine-month desert experience. They seem to serve well as a gauge of how well my hermit experience has actually gone. These were his suggestions:

1. Become friends with those demons that seem capable of conversion. Recognize them as plaguing society as well as your own soul, so that in honestly facing them, you do a service both to yourself and to others.

2. Learn which demons are best not engaged with alone, or not at this time.

3. Heal the memories that flood back upon you by reexperiencing them from the perspective of God's forgiveness and acceptance. That will make it possible for you to forgive yourself.

4. Have a community that is praying for you, and have as well some individuals who have your pilgrimage high on their list of priorities, praying for you. The daily Eucharist will be able to sustain you with Presence along the way, so that you will not be alone, even in your aloneness.

5. Have a monastic rhythm to fall back on, such as the daily offices, so that you do not get lost in your own neurotic self.

6. Keep a sense of humor, especially about yourself—because God does.

7. Learn that even your negative traits are ways of knowing God. If you are compulsive, attribute compulsivity to God, for God is totally addicted to you. Correlatively, if you have a negative experience of God, discover in it something about yourself, for you will most likely dislike in others what you most fear in yourself.

8. Introduce your "child" to what you are doing now, thereby learning more about why that child keeps getting lost, and how he can best be nurtured.

9. *Learn the names of the different parts of you: left brain, right brain, stomach, the unconscious, the superego. And in the midst of the circus that they put on each day, be able to call each by name, just as a teacher oversees recess. Let a mantra emerge from whatever game they happen to play that day, thereby providing a "faith-purpose" for the whole. Gradually, as your ego loses control and abandons center stage, laugh—for you are being drawn into the Divine Ego in the darkness at the top of the tent.*

10. *Invite everything in your hermitage to become a sacramental, thereby functioning as spiritual guides—even the mouse who has a persistent yearning for your nonpersistent rice.*

11. *Your quest is not to seek the love of God, but to get out of the way of the God who already loves you. Be like a child securely loved on your parents' lap, until you find that you can enjoy yourself, too.*

The similarity between this road map and the actual terrain of my pilgrimage is satisfying. After Lauds, I walk intentionally into the driving wind. With hair amiss and eyes smarting, I savor myself as a truly happy person. I know now what the poet G. M. Hopkins knows of the "dearest freshness deep down things." I must never forget that the reason why my struggle has been so long and so difficult is that I am a dedicated extrovert, while many of the spiritual saints were introverts. Thus how foreign to me is the insistence of a desert father such as Arsenius, who insists that when a person of prayer "hears the song of a little sparrow, his heart no longer experiences the same peace. Even the movement of dry reeds in the wind is a distraction." No way—not so for this wind-blown extrovert. For me, God is sacramental, historical, sexual, relational, carnal, and ecstatic. And so from now on, may I be a monk in the world, with my hermitage always having a window opening out onto creation, textured by the promises of the God who specializes in the lost-and-found.

Saturday, January 3

Sometime last night, snow began, insulating the world with silence. By dawn, there are several inches. To my disappointment, I discover that I do not have any boots. Furthermore, the sneakers I am wearing have holes in both toes. Yet I find neither factor sufficient reason for staying indoors. So with each shoe and foot tied inside a plastic bread bag, I enter that rare moment of being the first footprints in a new world. White cedars watch like frozen scarecrows. I marvel at my guest status, walking into the silence within the Silence.

At twilight, I draw a deep tub of hot water, light three candles, and say Compline by heart, with Mozart as accompaniment. To be alone in a warm hermitage, tucked in by snow gently fingering the windows, is an answer to most questions.

Tuesday, January 6

Today I continue to discern what I have learned during these past months. By early evening, with more than sufficient notes recording my ponderings, I am ready to draw some *observations about where I am now in regard to my desert experience.*

1. The temptation to revert. *I am aware that as my remaining days in the hermitage grow shorter, the pressure to do is beginning to nibble at my being.* The first sign is that my *periods of contemplation are becoming self-shortened. And during Eucharist, I begin "saving time" by speed-reading the liturgy. In walking to the lake, I am in a hurry to get there. And once there, I am anxious to return. Even more damning is the temptation for this dynamic to become a barometer of self-esteem. Although I feel well anchored in my new life of living for its own sake in the now, an old demon has begun to ask: "What good does all this do?" Another chants, "Results are what count." And still another proposes the need for the approval of others concerning what I have been doing; otherwise it is meaningless. Yet, for the most part, I am able to say firmly to my talking self, "Sit quietly and savor being alive. You are on the edge of losing the pearl of great price which has found you." I will need the disciplines I have learned to help me hold on during these temptations until the quieter moments of nurturing can return. Those moments tend to be the little joys that make all the difference—a Bach fugue by firelight, a gentle rain on the roof, ascending the stairs by moonlight.*

2. Spiritual Direction. *I have learned the importance of having a spiritual director. Thus, for example, when I noticed the above tendencies, I confessed them to my director and received this letter by return mail:*

> *I see that in spite of your monastic schedule, you are like most other Christians. The first thing that disappears is*

contemplation. But it is good that you have noticed it, and want to do something about it. You must take at least twenty minutes in the morning and in the evening for contemplation, making it the most urgent "work" you do. I know you well. You are not quiet by nature. What is hopeful is that you do yearn for such quiet. God doesn't need to be found. God already lives in your depths. Let go and remain there. This letter is to sting your already stung conscience. Remember that you have entered the hermitage not to accomplish anything, but to let the Spirit teach you how to be. So go sit in the sun and tell all your work to "go to pot."

His wisdom confirms the characteristics of good spiritual directors. They must themselves have suffered, have drunk deeply of silence, contain a hunger for God within a restless heart, and have a community that radiates to them the unconditional love of God. Put simply, they must know the desert— and have survived.

3. Humor. During these months, laughter over the little things has become an unexpected gauge of my spiritual health. I found one particular journal entry that characterizes this emergence. It has to do with a gift sent for my birthday:

I opened the package from my daughter. It was a moose with pink plastic antlers. It has a story. Several years ago a friend sent it in remembrance of our canoe trip together in the boundary waters, where I saw my first moose. Was this pink plastic version a joke? A sacramental? Whatever, it remained carefully out of sight. But when Christmas came, it asked to become a gift to one of my daughters, the one whose strange sense of humor she blames on heredity. Her instant response was gratifying: "This has to be the ugliest thing I've ever seen." So here I am, trying to be a pious hermit, and here comes this pink moose by parcel post for a return visit. Right now it is just staring at me, with one antler sadly drooping. But tomorrow it will take a return trip in an oversized box, back to its rightful owner. I worry, but not much, how a moose with baby-pink antlers will fare in New York.

4. Playfulness. *I recall a one-sentence story by a friend. "The day my older sister stopped playing dolls with me was the day my dolls stopped talking." When there is no one with whom to play, loneliness sets in. Even clouds stop painting pictures. When I first came to the hermitage, I could not enjoy things because I had no one with whom to share them. But the hermitage has become a sacred place whose walls give me permission to be childlike. The primary ingredient in play is the enjoyment of doing something for its own sake. Then everything begins to talk. And in so doing, they, in turn, witness to the fact that I am not alone.*

5. Poetry. *These months have evoked a rebirth of poetry in me. Neither abstract academic language nor everyday talk seems right for the desert. More appropriate are the sounds of the poet as lover. Last fall I chose William Butler Yeats for reading. One morning he came along to one of my favorite places: a log beside a humble stream, one that slightly gurgles rather than runs. I opened the book. The first glance was a discovery that he admires those who "at dawn drop their cast at the side of dripping stone" (The Tower). After returning to the hermitage, I read more. Yeats confesses wanting to build "a*

small cabin" so that he can have peace there, for "peace comes dropping slow." In such a place he could "hear lake water lapping with low sounds by the shore . . . in the deep heart's core" (The Lake Isle of Innisfree). He has been here.

6. Conviction. Faith has taken on an heroic quality. In these modern times of subjectivity and impulse feelings, there is something sacred about words of promise and of commitment, such as the conviction that "no matter what, this I will do." I found a journal entry that captures this in terms of the first vows taken by one of my monastic brothers.

The celebration of vows is simple, but powerful. After an opening prayer, the Abbot gives a homily, indicating that God is gentle, knocking before asking, and asking before entering. God's favorite dwelling place is in one's deepest self. Therefore the monk, in lying on the floor in the shape of a crucifix, is answering the knock, indicating an empty house, swept and ready for occupancy. And even if we do open the door, the Abbot cautions, all we can do is invite God in. We cannot force him to lease the space. But when God accepts the invitation, the monk enters a hidden life, not needing to be known or even seen, content instead to be led. Such a life parallels most of Jesus' own years, secret and hidden, about which only God knows. The Abbot declares that what a monk is called to do is to internalize the desert, entering a closet life with God, taking the world into one's silence as an intercession. When the homily ends, the monk comes forward, prostrating himself in a cruciform posture before the Abbot. He is asked what he seeks. Then he rises, and gives away his life. Perhaps there will come a moment when I shall be ready to do the same.

7. Community. *It has been said that there is no salvation outside the Church. Perhaps, but what is certain is that there is no way through the desert without a community providing support and accountability. During these past months, my monastic community has sustained me.*

8. Apprenticeship as a Spiritual Director. *The deeper I go into the desert experience, the more my mail resembles correspondence appropriately addressed to a spiritual director. The questions I am being asked seem less concerned for answers and more a longing for companionship in the struggle. And so my responses to those who write tend to be assurances that they are neither weird nor alone in their seeking. There seems to be a growing number of persons who need the crisis that only the desert experience can enable.*

9. The Future. *Having struggled there nine months simply to live in the now, I am puzzled as to what to do with the future. What am I to do with this desert experience, especially in the light of my commitment to social justice, as well as the frantic urban doing characterizing my former way of life? Put another way, has my living of this new lifestyle really brought clarity about why I entered the desert silence in the first place? By midnight, my thoughts congeal around two themes. First, more than I ever suspected when I began, I entered the desert to find* unconditional love and acceptance. *Some time ago, I wrote a one-line prayer to say when my digital watch sounded on the hour. It captures this theme better than I knew when I wrote it, expressing more of a yearning these than a conviction:*

Faithful Emmanuel, send us forth into your world, knowing that in your Spirit we will never again be alone, nor powerless,

*nor unaccepted, nor rejected, nor abandoned, nor of no conse-
quence, nor without meaning—for you indelibly are with us.*

*The test as to whether or not I am truly trusting that
acceptance will be the degree to which envy is absent from my
life. Thus far, I am doing well.*

*The second reason I now recognize for entering the desert
is directly related to my new future.* I want to drink deeply
the remaining time of my life, with an integrity that is
centered in refusing either to give up or to give in. *This
emerging faith-style will need to alternate the rhythms of city
and hermitage, the dispositions of extrovert and introvert, the
call to social justice and to contemplation—and thus balancing
the temperaments of doing, of having, and of being.*

Wednesday, January 7

*I seem to be reverting already. This morning my thinking
becomes so internally noisy that I call the monastery in the slim
hope that I can consult with my spiritual director. Surprisingly,
he is at the monastery gathering weekly leftovers for his meals.
As we listen to each other, the idea of alternating my two
lifestyles emerges. I would spend six months of my life as a
professor, living in the inner city and working with the poor.
During the other six months, I would be a monk, sharing my
time between the monastery and my hermitage. His final
comments are direct questions.* "Can you live on half-salary?"
"Yes." "Who is keeping you from doing this—parents?"
"They're dead." "Relatives?" "Far away." "Family?" "They
want for me whatever I want." "Colleagues?" "Most of them

would miss me." The only blockage turns out to be me. "So what mask is your desert demon wearing today?" "The one who says, 'How can you justify such uselessness as other than waste, irresponsibility, or failure?'" He correctly identifies my "doing demon." We conclude with a prayer, both of us promising to pray for illumination. Then he wisely reminds me: "In the end, the resolution is not ours to make." "Right."

Today has been a long one. It is past midnight. I confess fright over the deep changes the Spirit has effected in me through the desert experience—and clearly has yet in mind.

Friday, January 9

This is my last night here at the hermitage. I need a final look at the stars. When the world has its top off, one can see forever. With happy tears, I recall younger years, when some of us slept on the roof of a cabin in the Colorado Rockies on August nights. We counted shooting stars to keep from sleeping, determined to miss nothing. During the intervening years, however, my experiences of violence and evil and death have tended to alienate me from nature. But now, with the new image of God forged in the desert, I feel a reunion with those earlier times. No longer is nature the problem, with history the hoped-for solution. Nor is humankind any longer the riddle, with God the answer. Nature and history and God and humankind, all of us together, are one wild continuum. We are in it together, Milky Way and all—going for it.

There is sadness in doing each thing as if for the last time. Motionless tonight at the hermitage door, I feel the pain of this being my last night to be ravished by the silence. Even to open the door would be the sin of sound. Finally I do, and walk outside into the inside of everything that was, and is, and ever shall be.

Saturday, January 10

This afternoon I must leave. I feel close to Simone Weil who preferred the absence of God to the presence of all else. The Absence of the presence with which I began this desert experience has become for me at least the Presence of the absence. I am a marked person, branded by Silence, without and within, and there is no way back.

As a hermit, the reason for my being must center in contemplation. And so I spend this final morning trying to appropriate what contemplation has actually come to mean for me. I can characterize it best as those ecstatic times when my unity with creation becomes so deep that my selfhood is dissolved into God as creation's Source and Dynamism. I no longer seek contemplation as if it were a unique or rare experience to discover. Instead, it is an identity to be evoked any time, anywhere, in relationship with anything. In such moments, I sense myself as God's embodiment. Put succinctly, God is in us as we become us in God. Through this expansion of consciousness, our identity, too, is deepened as a homecoming into the fullness of God. With such intensity comes the passion to empty everything I am and have into God's becoming, returning the gift of God's talents—with interest. The gifts most pleasing to God are variations on the theme of reconciliation with and care for every "jot and tittle" of God's creation.

I confess surprise at what I just wrote. For years I have denied having any direct experience of God. But just now I described what it is like at first hand. It has taken so long to grasp that the issue, after all, has not been the absence of the experience. It has been my inability to name the name. My last mail delivery brought a letter from a pastor who confessed his envy in hearing a young minister describe her experience of God as she celebrated her first communion.

Why don't such experiences ever happen to me? I will soon receive a doctoral degree for having an above-average knowledge of ideas about God. But my friend knows God. Every Sunday when I preach, it scares me half-silly. I know, but they don't, that while assuring others that God exists, I cling only to a hope that it is so.

His question has long been my own. I must reply, realizing that whatever I say will actually be a message to myself. Sitting in the gentle morning sun, I watch as my words tumble out spontaneously. They begin by recalling saints who, having God-experiences, insist that faith dare not be based on them. Such experiences are the first to be consumed by doubt's dark night. Jesus makes quite clear the heart of faith, in contrast with Thomas's insistence on experience: "Blessed are those who believe but have never seen." I pause as to feel the deep peace from what I just wrote. Faith can never be other than a gamble, followed by living as if. That is what makes faith graceful—it is the paradoxical courage emerging from the gift of being healed. My conclusion writes itself: "I no longer regret the Absence. This is what gives faith the heroic quality that I admire—as the commitment to live this absence as Presence."

The moment of leaving has come. Standing sadly now on the porch of my hermitage, padlock in hand, I recall a favorite cover from The New Yorker. It is the view of a bleak winter ocean as seen from the porch of a boarded-up summer cottage. A forgotten red sand-pail is the only object in sight, tenuously balanced on the banister. I always hoped that the child would remember it and return. I stand quietly at my hermitage door— hesitating, hoping, promising. Then I go back inside, searching for my own pail. I put it on the banister of the porch. Then with surprising peace, I drive up the road, turning only once for a final look at a lonely red pail that continues to beckon from the porch rail.

$$\mathscr{U}$$

It is evening now. This is the inner city. I am tired. The street noise makes clear that the desert will have to be portable. Near the end of his life, Merton was encouraged by the Tibetan spiritual masters to combine solitude and compassion. Their suggestion was that he be a hermit for part of the year, and then "come out for a while." Had Merton lived longer, I believe he would have modeled what seems to be emerging in me as a new form of spiritual living.

For Compline, I am drawn to my bedroom window. In the corner of the sill is a dry nest, where a mother dove once tried to teach a dead bird to sing. In the other corner is a new nest. Out beyond the rooftops, city lights are coming on, much as stars do. And in the growing darkness, I know what matters—that in me a once-dead bird is singing.

Epilogue

In the months that followed, I had to lay claim to the fact that whatever I would do and wherever I would go from that point on, I would do so as a hermit. There are more hermits living invisibly in our hills and cities than I ever imagined. I asked one of them to put in his own words what such a life is like for him, so that I might compare it with my own. This is his response:

I live without power from a plug, water from a faucet, heat from a thermostat, and light from a switch. Returning with tears to my hermitage after a trip to the city, all it takes is for me to light the lamp, stoke up the fire, set the teakettle to singing, and thank God for having this simple cabin as my home. So much of what had mattered before seems suddenly unimportant now. I wrote in my journal about sensing and feeling the silence, and about sounds in the night. I wrote about smells— about fire as a brother and how I learned to live with him. I wrote about sister water. Cocreating beauty with the Creator and all creation has become an absorbing passion. My wilderness has blossomed. My desert has bloomed. I have been able to open all the old closets of my life and take the skeletons out and bury them. I

*learned then that we hermits are people who know how
to glorify God by gardening, and cooking, and baking,
and building. We are those who are in love.*

In response to friends who continue to question me,
and inspired by Merton's efforts, I try my own version of
what it means to be a hermit:

*There have always been persons who by temperament or
situation are alone in the midst of people, without understanding
why. But there are others, such as myself, who have lived active
and rigorous lives in the world, only to leave it all behind to
enter the desert Such a hermit vocation is not for the young, for
it dare not spring from either idealism or rebellion. Rather, there
comes a point where one simply becomes tired of pretenses and
games. A thirst for integrity takes over—a passion to undertake
the austerity of living in complete honesty, without conve-
nience, support, or distraction. This call into solitude entails a
pilgrimage into darkness and crucifixion, for it annihilates the
self one once knew and fostered. It is a lonely path, hidden from
the eyes of the world that neither knows nor cares, certain that
the hermit is a failure. Free from the lure of possessions, power,
and prestige, the contemplative life has no practical use or
purpose. Hermits are dependent on pure faith, believing that
being a hermit is what God would have them be. To walk into
the desert silence is to be stripped of certainty that one has an
answer to anything—until the questions that once plagued the
mind nestle in one's soul as friends.*

*One would hardly enter such a valley of shadows willingly.
Yet amid all the options one has, strangely, there is no choice.*

Nothing else matters except to be a person of prayer. And some day, in the gentle quietness, standing among the ashes of dreams and ambition, one may be blessed with the only certitude likely to be given—that to seek is to be sought, and to find is to have been found.

To be drawn into this dread solitude is really an invitation to keep company with God's loneliness, the God emptied in total identification with us—ignored, hidden, forgotten, and profoundly poor. And drawn by this Presence, the hermit stands with the rejected ones everywhere, sharing the joy of simplicity, and emptying all that one is and does into the becoming of God.

In one sense, the hermit life is for everyone, for the healing we all need inevitably requires time in the desert. On the other hand, the world needs those persons who are called to be hermits for life. Several years ago my hermit spiritual director was invited to become the chaplain of a Trappistine monastery. Our whole monastic community prayed about this, to discern if he should go. Our conclusion was this: "We need our hermit on the hill lest we forget why we are making fruitcakes in the valley." All of us need a hermit on the hill—as evidence that healing is possible, and that redeemed persons need little more than to grow old loving their God.

Postscript

What I have written to this point is my retrospective appropriation of my nine-month hermit experience, done one year after I thought it had ended. I wrote it just for me. But now, more than a decade later, I have finally consented to make this desert experience public. I dare to do so, to become vulnerable in the face of others, because I have been persuaded that many of you out there are caught in the same backwashes and dead-ends that have laced my own life. Let us treat each other gently, and embrace in hope.

My rocky pilgrimage did not end in leaving the hermitage that last day. To enter the desert is never to pass through unscathed. There is no way that I could walk away from what happened, as if its marks were temporary. Although I returned to the city, and although I taught and did inner-city justice work as before, it was never the same. The content of my doing did not change much. It was my being that had changed. At the root of all my doings, I craved the silence of the hermitage, for a thirst of another kind had claimed me. In due time, I sought permission from the seminary president to teach half-time at half-salary. The purpose was to have the remaining six months each year for shared living between my hermitage and my monastery, endeavoring to find home in all three settings. This arrangement finally became a reality three years after my desert year.

During the same period, I worked with my Abbot to formalize a relationship with the monastery that we called a "Trappist Family Brother." Paralleling the vows that a novice takes, my commitment was for a three-year period. Written and signed as a covenant, it was placed on the altar during mass—a token of my own flesh and blood lying side-by-side with those of Christ.

The traditional vows are obedience (including poverty and chastity), *conversatio morum* (conversion of lifestyle), and stability. My covenant involved the first two, but not the third—or better, the notion of stability was expanded to include part-time residency in my hermitage, which is not on monastic land.

This arrangement worked well, at first. But nearing the end of the third year of living this covenant, it became clear that such alternation of place and lifestyle was no longer resolving, but rather intensifying, the issue of my dual calling and dual worlds. One path seemed to remain. Thus in 1992, I reaffirmed my covenant as a "perpetual" one, vowing for life my calling as both monk and hermit, until at death I would be buried side-by-side with my monastic brothers. Further, I gave permission to my playful, creative side to begin doubling the size of my hermitage. This involved such enjoyable features as a hyperbolic parabola for a study, transverse beams and windows for a library, and the carpentry shop I have always wanted. Such expansion was my way of vowing with my hands that this hermitage would be the permanent home for my pilgrimage from that point on.

In 1993 I was ready. I took early retirement, and left both teaching and city. What I chose, or what chose me, was to be a bridge—holding together a hermit life as participant in the midst of Ozark poverty, with communal solitude in the hidden forests of the monastery. Actually being such a bridge is symbolic of my whole life, bridging Catholic and Protestant, ghetto and suburbs, coal mine and university. So it was to continue, in a number of ways. There was no way I could turn aside from social justice work. The focus simply became rural. I asked a number of persons living near my hermitage what person or agency they regarded as doing the best work with the poor. When their suggestions pointed to the same person and same agency, I promised her to create whatever supplemental services were needed to seal the holes in the safety net. This has meant three things: creating a volunteer transportation arrangement; giving from my income so that there will be significant funds in a checking account from which the staff and I can draw to assist the poor; and beginning a battered women's shelter. In addition, I wanted to discern one larger social justice task that I felt called to undertake. This resulted in becoming facilitator in forming a statewide coalition to abolish the death penalty. I experience this blending of hermitage and world most powerfully when in solitude at fireside I share by telephone with each condemned person on the night of his execution. My new life also involves doing spiritual direction, oriented toward those whose intensity of pilgrimage might benefit from my guidance. The time apart in my hermitage has also provided a creative context for writing articles and books. The pace of my daily life is gentle, and to make sure that I do not relapse again into the vicious vortex of doing, my days remain divided into the seven prayerful segments by the Daily Office.

The most significant gift of all came as a surprise. Starting with my first encounter with monasticism more than twenty years ago, my pilgrimage has increasingly moved toward the Eucharist as the central paradigm. Yet one piece was missing. Deep within me was the yearning to be a priest. The meaning of life and faith was becoming a call to lift into God's Becoming the body and blood of this world, with all its suffering and evil, for the sake of creativity as its sacred heart. And once offered up, all is transformed, graciously returned to nourish a physically hungry and a spirituality thirsty world.

On August 24, 1996, I was ordained a Roman Catholic priest. Few things have felt as right as when on that day I lay in cruciform fashion on the floor, enfolded by the chanting which invited thirty saints by name to be present. John Wesley was one of these, combining wonderfully my Wesleyan heritage with my Catholic piety. Assisted to my feet, I made the promise of my life. Then, with hands anointed in special oil, I became a priest, branded for life to stand as the personage of Jesus himself at the Eucharist. And at my first mass, I experienced what it means to celebrate the unspeakable mystery that joins heaven and earth, reality and hope, past and future, God and humankind—Absence and Presence.

July 1997 brought another large moment. I climbed a 14,000-foot mountain with my five daughters for the last time, a feat that with this special mountain had escaped us two times before. On the summit we embraced, recognizing without need for words the sadness of aging. This would be my last mountain. Before my desert year, had I been asked what portion of my life I would like to relive, my answer would have been blunt. None! But asked on that windswept peak, climbed from the far side of my desert experience, my response was equally strong and clear. I would be eager to live every bit of it again, this time self-consciously to the glory of God.

One final symbolic moment remains to be shared, providing balance to my venture at living. My journal has shared some of the sacred times with my spiritual director, particularly that special Christmas Eve in the tiny chicken-coop hermitage where he lived so joyously. There came a time when a new abbot thought it wise for him, because of his age, to leave the hill, residing instead in a place closer to the monastery. One rainy afternoon, with sadness, he left his hill. Months later, I asked if he had all he needed in his new hermitage. "No. I would like the tabernacle that is bolted into the wall of my old hermitage, right above my bed." So up the mountain I went, my trusty tools in a less-than-trusty knapsack. I anticipated how joyous it would be to spend some sacred moments there, looking out on the tumbling hills through the window, being surrounded by mellow memories. Such was not to be the case. I arrived only to find the door torn from its frame, the picture window smashed, the potbelly stove stolen, and the walls covered with graffiti.

So it is, and so it will be. In order not to become unduly romantic regarding things spiritual, we must never forget that there will always a desert—for in this life we deal not only with flesh and blood, but powers and principalities. I fought back tears as I descended my hermit's hill. But grasped tightly in my arms, I carried the tabernacle of Presence.

It seems inappropriate any longer to call my life an adventure. On my last birthday a friend asked, "What are you looking forward to in the next year?" Most of my life I would have noisily answered. But on that day, well into the new century, I had no answer. I wanted simply to live fully that day, just as I had the day before, needing nothing more.

So I close, offering up my desert journal and the account of my appropriation of that experience. Let its benediction be a letter my hermit on the hill sent for me to read on the first day of my early retirement, as I turned from the desert toward my new life beyond.

The die is cast. You have officially been granted your retirement. Your hand is on the plow. You can no longer look back, lest you be not worthy of the Kingdom. For three years you have spent six months of each year in a life of prayer and study. Now you will be devoting yourself entirely to a life of prayer. Whatever you read, study, or do should be done to open your heart to prayer. And whatever writing you do should flow out of your heart of prayer. As the psalmist says, "Gather us from among the nations that we may thank your holy name, and make it our glory to praise you."

That is what your life is all about now—to thank and praise. And in so doing you will end up as the hermit on the hill for us all.

Endnotes

Chapter 1

1. W. Paul Jones, *The Province Beyond the River: The Diary of a Protestant at a Trappist Monastery* (New York: Paulist Press, 1981).

2. Arthur John Gossip, "But When Life Tumbles In, What Then?" in *The Protestant Pulpit,* ed. Andrew Watterson Blackwood (Nashville: Abingdon-Cokesbury, 1957), 204.

Chapter 2

1. Henry David Thoreau, *Walden* (Princeton: Princeton University Press, 1989), 89.

2. Edward M. Hays, *Prayers for the Domestic Church* (Easton, KS: Shantivanam House of Prayer, 1979), 119f.

Chapter 3

1. *The Liturgy of the Hours* (New York: Catholic Book Publishing Company, 1975), v. IV.

2. John Clark, O.C.D., *Story of a Soul: The Autobiography of Thérèse of Liseaux* (Washington, D.C.: Institute of Carmelite Studies, 1975), pp. 211–214, 270–271.

3. May Sarton, *Journal of a Solitude* (New York: W.W. Norton, 1992).

4. Charles Joseph Cummings, "Spirituality and Desert Experience," unpublished Master of Arts thesis, Duquesne University, May 1977.

Chapter 4

1. Carl Michalson, *The Witness of Radical Faith* (Nashville: Tidings, 1974), 93–94.
2. Matthew and Dennis Linn, S.J., *Healing of Memories* (New York: Paulist Press, 1974).

Chapter 5

1. Richard Rolle, "The Love of God," in *The Cell of Self-Knowledge* (New York: Crossroad, 1981), 113–120.
2. Abhishiktananda, *Prayer* (Philadelphia: Westminster Press, 1947).